When You Find Yourself in the
Belly of a Whale

Beth C. Whittington

Copyright © 2008 by Beth C. Whittington

When You Find Yourself in the Belly of a Whale
by Beth C. Whittington

Printed in the United States of America

ISBN 978-1-60477-939-4

All rights reserved solely by the author. The author guarantees all contents are original and do not infringe upon the legal rights of any other person or work. No part of this book may be reproduced in any form without the permission of the author. The views expressed in this book are not necessarily those of the publisher.

Unless otherwise indicated, Bible quotations are taken from The Holy Bible, New Living Translation. Copyright © 1996 by Tyndale House Publishers, Inc., Wheaton, Illinois 60189. Used by permission.

www.xulonpress.com

IN MEMORY OF NAN PETERSON

In the spirit of Paul (2 Timothy 4:7-8),
she fought a good fight.
She finished the race, she remained faithful, and she
did so with more grace, dignity, and purpose than
anyone could have imagined.
Nan died in the spirit in which she lived.

CONTENTS

Don't Just Stand There…Say Something 13
I'm a Christian; I'm Not Supposed to Be Scared.
    Wrong! 16
They Are All The Same, or Are They?...................18
Across the Porch 21
Etched in Stone 25
Whoever Said Life Is Supposed To Be Fair?.........29
God's Computer 31
"How Are You?" "I'm fine." 34
Read the Last Chapter First....................................36
The Yard Sale 40
Easier Said Than Done...42
Keeping Score 45
Roller Coasters Never Were My Favorite Thing ...48
How Do They Do That?...51
Sometimes It Flies, Sometimes It Stands Still 53
That Is So—God!..56
I Lied To the Man...58
I'm Sorry, God 61
Why Didn't You Answer, Lord? 63
The Night Shoot 67
It Can Soothe the Soul 70
A Calmness That Is Beyond Human
    Comprehension 73

That's Not Me In the Mirror 76
I Thought That Verse Was Reserved
   For Funerals 80
God Doesn't Deal In Percentages 82
Facts Versus Feelings 84
I Used To Raise My Eyebrows, Too 85
How Not To Be Eaten By a Lion 87
Spiritual Time Out 90
Put Your Feet in First 92
And God Said...What Did The Doctor
   Diagnose? 96
A Fish, A Plant, A Worm, and a
   Scorching Wind 100
The Issue We Don't Want To Discuss 104
The Hidden Baby 109
Please, Father, Just One Set Of
   Footprints Today 112
Footprints 115
It's A Two-Way Street 116
Keep On Writing! Keep On Calling! 119
The Diversion Tactic 122
The Slide Show 124
Manna 127
Trees Walking Around 131
The Duties Incumbent Upon Me 133
I'm Not Believing My Ears 138
Battle Ready? 142
Death By Gunshot 144
What's The Price On Your Head? 147
Networking 150
Complimentary or Contradictory? 154
Put Out To Pasture 159

Now, That's A Scary Thought 162
Hook, Line, and Sinker 165
The Sound Of Silence 169
It's In Black and White 172
This Is Not The Life I Signed Up For 174
Cat and Dog Perspectives 179
Oh, God! 184
Land of the Giants 187
Great Is They Faithfulness 191
All Is Well—At Least On The Inside 195
So You Will Know 198
Chartreuse 201
RSVP Today If Possible 204

ACKNOWLEDGMENTS

- Natalie, **Mom, Lesley,** and Buster: Thanks a million for proofreading *When You Find Yourself in the Belly of a Whale*.
- **Dad**: I value your theological input.
- **Becky**: I am grateful for your editing *When You Find Yourself in the Belly of a Whale*. I am eternally grateful that you spared me the grammar lessons that explained the necessity of the corrections!
- **Mom, Dad, Ashley, and Adam**: You are the light of my life! I treasure the faith I have inherited and pray that I have adequately passed it on.
- **Buster**: You are truly a gift from God. You are a man after God's own heart. How blessed I am to have such physical, emotional, and spiritual support in you!
- **Sistahs**: I know God has a sense of humor when I look at the blessings he has given me in you! What prayer warriors you are.
- **Extended family, friends, acquaintances, and people I've not yet met who have prayed me through trying times**…thank you from the bottom of my heart.

DON'T JUST STAND THERE...SAY SOMETHING

It's the strangest thing. There must be some smell or glow or something that emits from your body when you are going through difficulties. People seem to sense it. They catch your eye then seem to trip over themselves heading the other direction. Why? They simply don't know what to do or what to say. It is so easy for us to take their actions personally when we're wearing our emotions on our sleeve. They really mean nothing adverse by their inaction. In fact, many of them hurt deeply for you. Their pain on your behalf paralyzes them for a time. I base that on the fact that I had two dear personal friends to call several weeks after my cancer diagnosis. Both admitted that they knew about it but were too devastated to call. Their inability to deal with it emotionally at the time prevented them from calling sooner. They couldn't very well call to offer their support when they were slinging snot themselves!

Others don't run. They just pretend as though life were clicking along like it did yesterday—normal—whatever normal is.

Both of you can relax if ***you*** bring up the hurt at whatever level you choose. Until you do, those who care so deeply are at a loss to know whether inquiring will help you or hurt you. So, don't just stand there, say something! This applies to families of the one going through the difficulty, as well.

I realize that some are very private about things of this nature. Certainly that is your prerogative. The way I figure it, the more people praying, the better. I hope God has to put another angel on the incoming line on my behalf (just kidding!). Allow me to share my personal feelings; failure to share your pain cheats others out of being able to share your burden. I'm not talking about taking out an ad in the local paper. I'm referring to your personal friends and co-workers (realizing they are not always one and the same). I have always been a strong, organized, do-it-yourself kind of person. It was not my nature to be on the receiving end, and quite frankly, it was a little difficult at first, emotionally. Physically, I had no choice. When we're debilitated in any way, we need a support system more than ever. Sure, you've got God, but who do you think put those people in your path? It is my prayer that these writings will help you find peace and hope. But if I had not shared my feelings, you would not be reading this today.

You can use your pain to bring emotional and spiritual healing to others. ***You can be a blessing!*** Remember, though, blessings sometimes wear disguises. Look at Job. What about Joseph, when he was sold into slavery? And then there is Mary, the mother of Jesus, pregnant and unmarried. Each waited patiently and God did accomplish his purpose through them.

✧ "Mary responded, 'I am the Lord's servant, and I am willing to accept whatever he wants.' " -Luke 1:38(a)

I'M A CHRISTIAN; I'M NOT SUPPOSED TO BE SCARED. WRONG!

As humans, we have insecurities. It is comforting to know that some of those from the Bible that we consider to be in the Christian Hall of Fame weren't superhuman. They had fears and weaknesses just as we do. Check out Paul in I Corinthians 2:3. "I came to you in weakness, timid and trembling." The original word for weakness actually meant physically ill. You know, it's when you get that queasy feeling in the pit of your stomach or that lump in your throat, like when your doctor tells you what you fear the most. Fear, in the Biblical context, can mean literal fear or it can mean "to stand in awe" or "reverence" of. To me, Paul was outright scared! Trembling can't mean but one thing. He was shaking in his sandals—or, at least, he had a whole swarm of butterflies in his stomach.

Paul was scared another time. He was reluctant to say what he needed to say in Corinth because he was afraid they would kill him. The Lord unfolded plans for the next year and a half of his life through a vision. The Lord instructed him, "Don't be afraid!" (Acts 18:9) Preach it. And he said it in red letters in my Bible.

According to what I read in the Bible, it's okay to be afraid. But God doesn't want us to set up camp in the land of fear. Many times our perceived fears are worse than the actual threat we fear. God promises peace in the midst of our fears, no matter what the circumstances, if we run to him. Rev. Adrian Rogers said that "peace is not the absence of problems in life but the addition of (God's) power." It requires faith made of "spiritual steel and concrete" rather than "eggshells."

When we are afraid but continue to trust in God—that is when he often accomplishes his best through us.

To Live Is Christ, Beth Moore, LifeWay Press, Nashville, TN 37234, 1997, p100.

THEY ARE ALL THE SAME, OR ARE THEY?

Carcinoma. Melanoma. Melodrama! I had no clue as to the difference.

A chicken snake, I am told, is a good snake. We shouldn't kill that kind. Now if you ask me, a snake is a snake is a snake! The only good snake is a dead snake.

Sometimes things that initially seem 100% wrong are found, eventually, not to be all that bad. The loss of a job, a wrong turn in a relationship, having your car totaled or a debilitating health diagnosis. Do I have the right to talk about it? You bet I do! Lumpectomy, mastectomy, chemo, weight loss, hair loss (including eyebrows and eyelashes), and depression.

Carcinoma. Cancer. What on earth could be positive about having cancer? Nothing! Absolutely nothing was my initial reaction (initial meaning several weeks). Friends were having people who had "been there and done that" to call me. I was reading everything I could get my hands on about it. Frankly, I didn't see anything positive that could come from such a diagnosis until I happened upon a book in the New Orleans International Airport. Stormie OMartian suggested in *Just Enough Light for the Step I'm On* that we look at adverse situations in a different light. Ask yourself, "What's right with this picture?" I realized that God had allowed me to find the malignancy in an early stage. It was treatable with good success rates. Because my daughter was serving as a summer foreign missionary, I was being prayed for by God-fearing people from two foreign countries as well as by friends, and friends of friends, from all over the United States. I was receiving a handful of encouragement cards each day. People that I didn't even know sent notes and testimonies of encouragement. I had accumulated a sufficient amount of sick time to see me through. My employer was extremely supportive, as was my family. I had good insurance, etc., etc., etc.! As time passed, I began to see God closing out some chapters of my life and opening some new ones.

I've wondered if God and Satan talked about this cancer thing and came to an agreement like they did with Job (Job 1:6-2:8). I've shuddered over the thought that maybe that was the only way God could get my attention. And I've pondered whether it was just one of those bad things that happens to good people.

In the Job story, though his friend Eliphaz was in error with his thought that the whole ordeal was because God was disciplining Job, he was correct in pointing out God's ability to deliver us from whatever.

Oh, and do you for one minute think I **happened upon** that book?

✧ "For though he wounds, he also bandages. He strikes, but his hands also heal. He will rescue you again and again so that no evil can touch you." -Job 5:18-19

Just Enough Light for the Step I'm On, Trusting God In the Tough Times, Stormie Omartian, Harvest House Publishers, Eugene, OR 97402, 1999.

ACROSS THE PORCH

My daughter, who is away in college, sent me one of the sweetest expressions of love. The card said, "If I could sit across the porch from God, I'd thank Him for lending you to me." And, she wrote, "Mom, thank you for praying for me. You're the best mom in the world. I couldn't have asked God for a better one."

In another card, she wrote, "Thank you for raising me in a real Christian home—for being an example of a godly woman." Instead of feeling pride, it took me to my knees. I thought of all of the things I had done wrong and others that I had left undone. Oh, if I could go back and do it again—to right the wrongs, to react differently, to be less busy, to worry less, to lecture less, to reach out more—but that chapter of my life is closed. Paul said, "I am still not all I should be, but I am focusing all my energies on this one thing: Forgetting the past and looking forward to what lies ahead" (Philippians 3:13). I am so thankful that God allowed us to raise two kids that are sold out to him, in spite of ourselves.

What about Jesus' relationship with his daddy? No doubt, they had the closest of relationships. In Mark's account of Jesus' agony in Gethsemane (Mark 14:32-36), Jesus told his disciples, "My soul is crushed with grief to the point of death. He went a little further and fell face down on the ground. He prayed that, if it were possible, the awful hour awaiting might pass him by. Abba, Father, he said, everything is possible in you.

Please take this cup of suffering away from me. Yet I want your will, not mine." Dr.

Luke tells us that Jesus was in such agony that his sweat fell to the ground like big drops of blood. Jesus shared his true feelings with his daddy. He understood what he was about to go through and he was asking if there were any other way that sinners could be saved than by his death, burial, and resurrection. If at all possible, he wanted to avoid the horror, the pain and suffering, and the separation from God that he was about to endure. Jesus didn't ask his Father just once. He went back into the garden two more times to plead with his Father. God didn't outright refuse to answer the prayer of his son. It's just that our Father knows best. He has the big picture.

I strongly identify with this passage. I find it to be a wonderful example of how to pray during trying times. There have been occasions that I have felt so undeserving of my Father's love and times that I have been extremely distraught over situations that were occurring in my life. I have literally prayed lying face down on the floor. This scripture teaches us to face reality and to be totally honest with God about how we are feeling. It speaks of being persistent in prayer. Jesus, just like us, kept on asking his Father to change the plan, but if that were not possible, he was willing to go the distance. He was so human at the time, yet so Divine.

Let's reverse the parent/child relationship and look at it from a different angle.

Think for a minute about our Heavenly Father. He loved us enough to send his only son to die to cover our sins, making us his children if we choose. He adopted us into his kingdom, giving us the same rights and privileges as a natural born child. He is our Abba (Aramaic for daddy). He loves us beyond measure. He cares about everything we say, do, and think. He only wants the best for us. He doesn't want us to worry. When we mess up, he doesn't kick us out of the kingdom. Rather, as our Father, he attempts to show us the error of our ways. When some tragedy knocks us down in life, he picks us up, dusts us off, and holds us for a while. How do I know? He told us through the numerous verses he has in his book, the Bible. And I've experienced the peace that comes from sitting on the porch with him.

We have to remember that our Father knows best. He has the master plan, and I don't want to be anywhere that is not a part of it. We all have but one life to live on this earth. There is no going back. I hope and pray daily that, even though I have been through an extremely difficult year battling cancer, I am only in the middle of my book of life. I, too, want this cup to pass from me, but, I am resigned to live life to its fullest, even though my body hurts, I'm hairless, and tired to the max! Cancer has caused me to take a physical inventory. I've said "yes" to too many things, so I've vowed to sincerely pray about every committee or activity I'm asked to serve on prior to accepting the position. I've been equally busy at home. I've promised myself that I will sit down and do **nothing** more each day. That one is awfully hard for me. Cancer caused me to take a spiritual inventory. I looked at life from every angle and I cannot tell you why cancer struck me. I've asked God to reveal any areas of my life in which I am not in line with him. I don't think that my illness was because of sin in my life, but because God wanted me to close some chapters of my life and open new ones.

One day maybe I can sit across the porch from God and he'll explain the "whys and why nots" of life. Probably not, though. By then, I'd rather be skiing down the heavenly Mount Sinai, fishing with my Uncle David on the Jordan, playing golf where there are no sand traps, singing with the choir, reuniting with friends and loved ones, looking up my grandparents, meeting Moses, Paul, Matthew, Dr. Luke, Peter and the boys, enjoying a body that doesn't ache, but most of all, truly worshipping my Lord.

Yes, I want this cup to pass from me. But I want more for my Father to be able to send me a card that says, "Well done, my good and faithful servant."

Card by Flavia Publishing Company, Santa Barbara, California

ETCHED IN STONE

REST—we so seldom get it. Let me remind you of what it is—freedom from activity or labor. I thought I was doing it until I looked up its definition. Being a Type A personality, as I began to get some of my strength back after chemo, you can imagine what happened. I over did it—too much activity zapped me. Even when I fell on the couch exhausted, I would read, work on the lap top computer, or grade papers. My husband, realizing what was happening said, "I want to see you sitting on the couch doing **nothing** more often." I don't "do nothing" well. I found that sitting on the couch working on my lap top doesn't fit the definition of rest—freedom from activity.

God told us, way back in Exodus (20:10), that one day a week was to be set aside for rest. We can change a lot of things in life but this one is etched in stone—literally.

Not once, but twice. Remember, God gave the Ten Commandments to Moses but when Moses came down from Mt. Sinai and found that the Israelites were engaged in pagan worship to golden calves, he broke the very tablets of stone on which God had inscribed the covenant. God made a duplicate set, front and back, that are still in effect today.

Let's zoom in on Aaron for a minute. It's easy for us to read from Exodus and get aggravated at him. In Chapter 19, Moses was on the mountain conversing with God. God sent Moses down to bring Aaron back up with him. In Chapter 24, Aaron, Moses, and seventy-two others went up the mountain but God instructed that they worship from a distance. Only Moses was allowed to go near God. All of them went down the mountain in order for Moses to deliver God's laws to the people. Then back up the mountain they went (makes me tired just thinking about mountain climbing), Moses, Aaron and his two sons, and the 70 religious leaders. They saw God with his feet on what appeared "to be a pavement of brilliant sapphire, as clear as the heavens." In fact, they shared a meal together in God's presence. Yet, God allowed them to live. Zoom in on Aaron. Just eight chapters later he has allowed the Israelites to con him into making a golden calf idol for them to worship. How could he do that? One day he is dining with God and a few days later his willful disobedience almost cost him his life.

Don't we do the same thing? God's command to rest has been in the Book for years, yet we willfully choose to ignore it. Actually, God's command says, "Remember to observe the Sabbath day by keeping it holy. Six days a week are set aside for your daily duties and regular work, but the seventh day is a day of rest dedicated to the Lord your God" (Exodus 20:8-10). God's commandment was for our benefit. He was concerned enough about us to provide a day each week to rest. As we observe a regular time of worship each week, we have the added benefit of refilling our spiritual cups. What a loving God to be that concerned about our physical and spiritual health!

There is another side to this story. Years later "The apostles returned to Jesus from their ministry tour and told him all they had done and what they had taught. Then Jesus said (in red letters, mind you), 'Let's get away from the crowds for a while and *rest*.' " Check this out. "There were so many people coming and going that Jesus and his apostles didn't even have time to eat." So, what's new? You would think that when they left in a boat they were home free, but apparently the townspeople had their binoculars out. They (many townspeople; vast crowds) "ran ahead along the shore and met them as they landed." It was just Jesus' nature to have compassion, teach them, and feed them.

He didn't just feed them, **HE FED THEM** with five little loaves of bread and two not-

so-big fish. The apostles, as well as the people, learned a valuable lesson that day.

God can do the impossible! One of the neatest miracles would not have happened if Jesus and the disciples had insisted on their rest and relaxation.

It seems as though this writing pulls us two different directions. ***To rest or not to rest—that is the question.*** Doing God's work is of utmost importance, but even Jesus recognized that to do it effectively we need periodic rest and renewal. My best friend, a nurse, reminds me to listen to my body. If I listen to my body and listen to my Lord, he will show me the happy medium.

- ✧ "Then Jesus said, 'Come to me, all of you who are weary and carry heavy burdens, and I will give you rest.' " -Matthew 11:28-30
- ✧ "He lets me rest in green meadows; he leads me beside peaceful streams. He renews my strength." -Psalm 23:1-3

WHOEVER SAID LIFE IS SUPPOSED TO BE FAIR?

We in America enjoy our groceries. It is just not natural to deprive our bodies of peas, cornbread, chicken, rice and gravy, apple pie, and sweet tea. Just as our bodies crave sustenance, so do our souls. Augustine noted, "You have made us, O Lord, for yourself, and our heart will find no rest until it rests in You." Jesus, himself, said in essence that we can drink from our bottles of water all day long, but we're just going to get thirsty again. But those who drink from the Living Water will not ever be thirsty again.

Our stay here on earth is not what was in the original master plan. Why? Because sin crept in. Therefore, life is not fair—never has been, never will be. It wasn't fair that Jesus had to be beaten and crucified for something I would eventually do. Think back to all that Paul endured (shipwrecks, death threats, hunger, jail.) Life is not fair, but the God who created us is so very fair. Do you remember what he put up with from the Israelites? Consider all of the chances he gave the people of Sodom and Gomorrah. And what about our own lives? The bottom line is that Solomon, who was wealthier and wiser than any of us can ever hope to be, tried to find happiness through things on this earth and failed. There is no need for us to learn it the hard way. In the midst of our trials we must seek God with all of our hearts—the totality of our being, total devotion. This is a commandment, not an option (Mark 12:30). We can question the fairness of life until the trumpet blows, but we'll be tired, worn out, bitter and angry if we do. God made us and he hasn't forgotten us. God knows about everything that happens in our lives even before we do. He never promised a life without hardships, but he did promise to be with us through the good and the bad. It's not like he jets in every now and then to check on us and see how we're holding up. He stands close beside us, and sometimes he even carries us, so that we can have peace in the midst of our storms.

✧ For a deeper study: Romans 8:35-38, 2 Corinthians 11:23-28, Matthew 22:37-39; *Believer's Bible Commentary*, William MacDonald, Thomas Nelson Publishers, Nashville, TN, 1995.

GOD'S COMPUTER

Just suppose that you had reached the age of accountability, meaning you realized that you were a sinner and asked Jesus into your heart so that you would live forever in his presence. Suppose God, at that point, invited you into his office for a conference. Imagine God going to his computer, getting on the Internet and pulling up different roads and trips and experiences and options that could be in your future. He gets up and goes to a rack on the wall and begins to pull brochures.

While you wait, you notice his screen saver—a door opening into heaven. It led to a throne made of brilliant colored gemstones. A ring of green light like an emerald circled the throne like a rainbow. There were twenty-four other thrones, with the same number of older men sitting on them. They all wore white and had gold crowns on their heads. Flashes of lightning and a rumble of thunder came from the main throne. Lamps with burning flames stood in front of the throne beside "a shiny sea of glass" that sparkled like crystal (Revelation 4:2-6). "Truly fascinating," you think.

Suddenly you are jolted back to reality as he places several brochures into your hand. He instructs you to take them home, peruse them, and get back with him next week with the ones that interest you the most.

Imagine that! Why do you think God doesn't consult us with the turn of events in our lives? Well, here is the deal. God's mission statement is often quite different from our own. He is zeroed in, totally focused, on the distant future. We would not likely choose the rocky, narrow path nor "the road less traveled." He wants us to experience things that we would never choose for ourselves. He wants us to soar to new heights, to live on a totally different plane, but to get there we must experience the bumps and jolts and the mountains and valleys in life.

"Turn your eyes upon Jesus. Look full in his wonderful face. *And the things of earth will grow strangely dim,* in the light of his glory and grace." I've always loved that old song. It means so much more to me than words on a page. Think about it. When we are totally focused on him, the detours don't seem like detours. He uses our adversities to allow us to help fellow Christians make it through the land mines in life. He will use us to introduce others to a much better way of life—one where our living Lord walks with us every step of the way. One who gives us direction at every turn.

I am reminded of my brother-in-law who lost his way while enroute to our house. He called and said, "Where am I?" With God, there are no wrong turns. He may take us site-seeing now and then. And we may view life from a few back roads.

My son usually has his own vehicle at church on Sunday evenings because his activities start much earlier than ours. One particular Sunday, however, our entire family of four actually rode together in the same vehicle! On the way home, we stopped at several car lots—car shopping. We didn't realize that anything was amiss until we walked into the house and couldn't find Adam. Poor baby! And it was Easter Sunday. I am so thankful that God never forgets where he has left me. Granted, sometimes it seems like he leaves us hanging, but God promised he would never leave us or forget us.

The neat thing about God's computer is that he can hit the *delete* button and in an instant wipe out the aftermath of all of the wrong turns in our lives and install a whole new program.

I know the Bible doesn't say anything about computers, but I was just wondering —do you think the *Book of Life,* the list of who has reservations in heaven, is computerized? Sure hope it's not *down* when I get to the pearly gates!

Turn Your Eyes Upon Jesus, Helen H. Lemmel, Singspiration Music, 1922, The Baptist Hymnal, Convention Press, Nashville, TN, 1991

"HOW ARE YOU?" "I'M *FINE*."

Fine is often used to mean quite well or excellent. Why do we feel compelled to say that when we are far from good physical and mental well-being? It could be that we know that the inquiring party really isn't interested in the full details. Or perhaps we feel the need to pretend that everything is all right. Maybe it is not the right time or place to discuss the nitty-gritty details. Or maybe we just don't know what else to say.

I had been diagnosed with cancer two days earlier when a friend and colleague asked, "How are you?" I said "Fine," of course. My mind immediately carried on a conversation with itself. "Why did you say that? You are not okay. You've got it together one minute and the next you are in tears." Close friends know how to read between the lines. They know when to gently pry into your business for your own well being with such comments as "how are you handling this?" or "how are you, really?"

Earlier that same day I was lying *in* a machine that was about to conduct a bone scan of my body. The attending nurse asked "are you doing okay?" You know my automatic response. As the machine began to move ever so slowly over the length of my body I told God "I AM NOT FINE! I am scared. I'm not scared of the machine but I am scared of what the machine might find." My body was calm on the outside, but it was doing some serious shaking on the inside.

I thought about the picture in my daughter's room entitled *"Watchers in the Night,"* in which the artist painted an angel guarding the bedside of a beautiful sleeping child. The angel stands at attention, with his wings almost totally surrounding the bed. In his left hand, he holds a spear. The other palm is cupped upward to emit a soft glowing light.

At that moment, the inner shaking of my body stopped. I knew that either God, Himself or one of his angels was in that nuclear medicine room with me. No, I never saw anybody but the nurse and me. I just knew. You see, when I 'fessed up to the Father, I was able to totally relax. I WAS FINE!

❖ "For he orders his angels to protect you wherever you go. They will hold you with their hands." –Psalm 91:11-12(a)

"Watchers in the Night," Artist Thomas Blackshear, II, MasterPeace Collection, DaySpring, Siloam Springs, AR, 1995.

READ THE LAST CHAPTER FIRST

Oh, come on! You've all done it, or at least thought about sneaking a peek at the last chapter of a book because you just had to know. You couldn't wait. Wouldn't it be neat if when babies were born they came with books, as in manuals? God could stick their biography in our mail box. As parents, we could check the book and take comfort in the fact that our children would make it through their adolescent years and eventually outgrow their teenage behavior and grow up to be responsible adults. We could check the final chapter and see that the crisis of the moment would be well worth it in the end.

God must have thought along these lines once. He gave us Revelation, which is in essence, the last chapter. We know who wins in the end. But in the game of life, we don't have the option of knowing how the crisis of the moment will turn out. That's where faith comes in. Sometimes I think we talk about faith a lot more than we understand it. *Pistis* the Greek word for faith, is used over 200 times in the New Testament. It can be used in several contexts. It is a gift from God that allows us to receive salvation (Galatians 3:16). It is God's grace (underserved favor), not the faith itself, that assures us of a place in heaven. After receiving salvation, it is through the faith that he gives that we learn to be more Christ-like. The more we use our faith, the stronger it gets. Why? Because we see God's faithfulness over and over again. We learn that we can trust him to keep his promises and see us through every situation that we face, even when we have no clue as to what he is up to or can't see how the situation could possibly turn out for the good (2 Kings 6:16-17). God's provisions are in direct proportion to our faith and willingness to obey (2 Kings 4:6).

It has been said that *faith is walking to the edge of all of the light you have and taking one more step*. Faith is more than just believing. It involves entrusting our lives. Picture the Flying Wilendas, the famous family of trapeze artists. We believe that they can walk across the tight rope and back again, but are we willing to let them carry us across? I don't think so! (For whatever it's worth, the family holds hands and prays before every performance.) Through faith, God provides spiritual resources that we cannot see. Elisha, the prophet, experienced a unique example of that (2 Kings: 16-19).

The king of Syria was extremely angry because his secret plans were repeatedly revealed to the king of Israel. When he learned that Elisha was the source of the revelations, the king set out to capture Elisha at all cost. He sent an army in the night to surround the city of Dothan, near Samaria. At day break, Elisha's servant was terrified when he saw the mighty army. God allowed Elisha a glimpse of a vast army of horses and chariots of fire, sent by God to protect his people. Furthermore, God struck the Syrian army with blindness, enabling Elisha to lead the entire army on to the city of Samaria.

We need to ask ourselves, "Is my faith real?" The Father said (Matthew 3:9-10) that God has no use for people who call themselves Christians, yet live a life in which others cannot see any evidence of their faith. He compares them to trees that do not produce fruit, therefore are cut down and thrown into the fire. If others cannot see evidence of our faith, we may not be children of God.

Suffering in this world, whether physically or emotionally, in and of itself is not a test of our faith. God's word makes it clear that suffering is a part of the human life.

There are countless examples of godly people who suffered. On the other hand, suffering does test our faith. We either become stronger in our faith or we blame God and turn away from him.

If you are wrestling with the understanding of faith, take comfort in the fact that Billy Graham doesn't totally understand it either. He said, "I do not understand the digestive system, but I eat. I don't understand about our respiratory system, but I continue to breathe. So it is with faith. We cannot understand all things. We must have faith."

Biblical Cyclopedic Index, *The Open Bible,* New Living Translation, Thomas Nelson, Inc., Wheaton, Illinois, 61089, 1998.

Life Application Bible, New International Version, Tyndale House Publishers, Inc., Wheaton, Illinois 60189, 1996.

Touch Point Bible, Holy Bible, New Living Translation, copyright 1996. Used by permission of

Tyndale House Publishers, Inc., Wheaton, Illinois 60189.

THE YARD SALE

Once upon a time we were snow skiing in Colorado with friends. Ski trails are named and color-coded on the signs and maps so that skiers will know the difficulty of them. We had stopped at the very edge of one trail so we could lay our eyes on the slope to see for ourselves how steep it was when, suddenly and simultaneously, Nan and I began to slide, fall, tumble, and roll hopelessly out of control for what seemed like forever. Thirty minutes later, when we finally stopped, most of what we had previously worn on our bodies was strewn about the mountain for all to see. Our stuff was scattered for miles, or so it seemed—caps, gloves, skis, poles—just like in a yard sale.

As a result of that experience, today Psalm 121:3 has taken on a new meaning!

"He will not let your foot slip." I know that as I tumbled, I prayed for a tree to stop us.

God knew that a tree would likely kill us or cause great bodily injury, so he didn't put one in our path. He was there on the mountain with us, protecting us the entire time.

Commentators of the Life Application Bible center the theme of Psalm 121 around the fact that we can depend on God for protection. That passage goes on to say that "he who watches over you will not slumber nor sleep," or as my pastor put it, "God never sleeps or dozes off." During the wee morning hours, after midnight, when we are dead to the world, he is constantly watching over us, protecting us from all evil. He never gets tired.

When I was diagnosed with cancer, life as I knew it changed rather abruptly. It is comforting to know, especially in times of uncertainty, that God, the Creator of everything, is still in charge. Nothing can divert his attention. Nothing, but nothing, is more powerful than he to handle our every need.

<<<<<<<<<<◇>>>>>>>>>>

Dr. B. David Brooks, Calvary Baptist Church, Alexandria, LA, June, 1996.

EASIER SAID THAN DONE

The university's indoor swimming pool is located just down the hall from my office. In fact, I use the pool entrance because it is a shortcut. Many times the water is still and the light reflects off its surface, giving the appearance of a highly waxed and polished floor. I'm reminded of Simon Peter almost every time I see it. I've considered gathering all of my faith and just walking across it. But since I don't bring extra clothes to work, I figured it was probably not in my best interest!

I admire Simon Peter's spirit. He was so gung-ho about everything he did—like the time he cut off the ear of Malchus, the high priest's servant, in an effort to protect Jesus and keep him from being arrested. His heart was in the right place, but many times he went about things the wrong way. When Jesus predicted his denial, Peter said, "Lord, I am ready to go to prison with you, and even to die with you," yet three days later, on three different occasions, he wouldn't even admit that he knew Jesus. Then there was the time that Peter exercised his faith and walked on the water. He was doing fine until he took his eyes off Jesus. He thought about what was happening and he noticed that the waves were rather high and crashing around him. He was terrified. The distraction caused him to lose faith so he began to sink. Putting faith into practice is easier said than done!

We know what Peter did wrong. But what did he do right? He immediately put his focus back on

Jesus. "Save me, Lord!" he shouted. And, Jesus grabbed him.

Then Jesus asked Peter, "Why did you doubt me?" (Matthew 14). Unfortunately, I can relate to that. During the time I was recuperating from cancer surgery and taking chemo, I received a get well card from my aunt in which she wrote, "How many times have I heard you say "I'm giving it to God?" She was reminding me to take my own advice—to remember that God had always been faithful, and that fighting cancer was not an exception to the rule. But you know, it is so much easier said than done, especially when you are the one walking on the water! It is so easy to take our eyes off our Heavenly Father and focus on ourselves. It is so easy to get pulled under by the waves of fear, depression, and pain. It is easy to ask "why me?"

Wouldn't you know, Peter asked that question, too. After his resurrection (John 21), Jesus appeared to seven of the disciples while they were fishing on the Sea of Galilee. As soon as Peter recognized Jesus, he jumped into the water and swam ashore. Notice, he didn't try the walking on water trick again. During this encounter, Jesus asked Peter three times, "Do you love me?" Bible scholars tell us that initially Jesus was referring to a self-denying, sacrificial love, but the third time he asked Peter, in essence, "Are you even my friend?" Peter was likely beating around the bush because of his insecurities over his recent denial of Jesus. Peter's actions, however, had not diminished Jesus' love. He had a plan for Peter to fulfill. Their conversation ended with Jesus revealing that after many years of ministry Peter would be crucified for his beliefs, but in so doing it would bring honor to God. Peter looked at John and asked, "What about him?" In other words, "why me?" Whether the question was asked out of curiosity or jealousy or in order to rationalize, we'll never know. We do know that Jesus admonished Peter not even to go there—not to compare his life with that of another.

There is not a place high enough, low enough, or far enough away that God doesn't know where we are and what we are experiencing. We tend to see life's adversities as being some form of punishment from God. We should never make that assumption. Our loving Heavenly Father often uses these situations to get our hearts and minds more in tune with his. Though it is certainly easier said than done, we must be in constant prayer for God to show us what to do, where to go, what to think, what to write, what to say, and to change anything within us that is keeping us from our divine calling. Oh, yes, you have been called if you are a Christian. The Bible says it, I believe it, and that settles it.

- "Show me the way in which I should walk and the things I should do." –Jeremiah 42:3 (NKJ)
- "And you will hear a voice say, "This is the way, turn around and walk here." –Isaiah 30:21

KEEPING SCORE

Have you ever noticed what a score-keeping society we have become? From the types of houses we live in, to the cars we drive, to our kid's report card grades, we try to keep up with the Jones family—whoever and wherever they are! Frequently, we are not happy campers when we spent our vacation in pitched tents and the Jones' went on a cruise. (Poor Jones. They've really gotten a bad rap over the years.) Before we know it, we can be wrapped up in our own little pity party.

That same mentality crosses over into our heath issues. We tend to compare our quality of life with those around us and sometimes lay blame where it does not belong. Some erroneously attribute repeated illnesses or "bad luck" to punishment for sin.

I guess the Jones lived back in the 1800's, too. At least that's when the song, *Count Your Blessings*, was written. I love the words of that old song:

"When upon life's billows you are tempest tossed,
When you are discouraged, thinking all is lost.
Count your blessings, Name them one by one,
And it will surprise you what the Lord hath done."

A blessing is God's free and unmerited favor toward sinful humanity. Have you ever stopped to count them and "name then one by one?"

If God took me back in time and allowed me to choose whether or not I would endure cancer, surgeries, and chemo, I would have to say "yes, I'll do it." (No, I'm not under the influence of any narcotic drug as I write this.) Already, it has been a life- changing experience for which I am grateful. No doubt, chemo wreaked havoc with my body. But, oh, the rewards! I have a closer relationship with friends, relatives, and co-workers. I have devoted Christian oncology nurses and doctors. People have been so generous to bring food, not just once or twice, but for six months. They have taken time out of their busy schedules to visit me, which in and of itself, is becoming a lost art. I have a large basketful of encouraging cards, letters, and emails. I have truly learned the value of friends. My best friends have been there for me every step of the way. Numerous friends that I had lost touch with over the years have called or written. I've been able to re-establish relationships with them. I relate to my heavenly father on a much deeper level. I have seen him change the direction of my life, and I like it. I'm not as busy doing "stuff." The cool crisp air of spring smells better than ever before. The birds sing louder. The sunsets are prettier. My insurance has paid well. I was able to continue to teach college half days, most of the time. He has allowed me to minister to others undergoing chemo. I didn't get yucky sick as much as many people do. I could go on and on and on. God is so good, all the time!

When faced with major decisions, my husband and I have had the practice over the years of listing all of the pros and all of the cons of the issue. Then, we've prayed about it and reached our decision. I would urge you to get a piece of paper and a pencil and begin to list your blessings. Better get a big piece! " It will surprise you what the Lord has done."

- "Let them praise the Lord for his great love and for all his wonderful deeds to them." – Psalm 107:31

Count Your Blessing, Words by Johnson Oatman, Jr.; Music by Edwin O. Excell. The Baptist Hymnal, Convention Press, Nashville, Tennessee.

ROLLER COASTERS NEVER WERE MY FAVORITE THING

Especially emotional ones. Life can be rolling along rather steadily one minute, and the next, it is upside down and headed in the opposite direction. At least with most roller coasters, you can see the turn coming, whereas in life there is often no advance warning. The strange thing about emotional roller coasters is that the triggering mechanism is usually not tangible. It is often not even the result of what someone said or did or didn't do that caused you to "lose it," but you find yourself crying, angry, or emotional for no real reason. That, coupled with a few other symptoms, like loss of appetite, being unable to sleep, acute anxiety, severe feelings of hopelessness, memory loss, and the inability to concentrate is called ***depression.*** I know. It's like a four letter word that you don't say. It is something that most people don't want to admit, much less, discuss. But it happens to all of us to some degree. It happened to me in the midst of three cancer-related surgeries, total hair loss, and all of the other side effects of chemotherapy. I have always been an in-control, organized, Type A personality, but this emotional roller coaster threw me for a loop.

It happened to various personalities in the Bible and God didn't see it as sin. In fact, he stood beside them and sometimes carried them through the dark days. David wrote in Psalm 130, "From the depths of despair (loneliness, isolation, hopelessness), O Lord,

I call for your help." In Psalm 39, he acknowledged that God knew everything about him. He could never sink so low in depression that he would be lost from God.

I would think that Job had some feelings of depression. And what about Paul? The tides were often turned against him. The Israelites (Numbers 11) gave Moses fits with their complaining; thus, Moses complained to God that he would rather be dead than put up with their constant complaining. Jonah prayed to die because he was emotionally distraught. Notice that death was not a part of God's plan, but seeing them through the difficulties was. Isaiah (53:3) speaks of Jesus as a "man of sorrows, acquainted with the bitterest grief." In other words, Jesus has been there and done that. He knows how we feel.

We tend to think that there is a flaw in our Christianity if we are depressed. We may feel as though we are being punished for not living up to God's expectations. The reality is that sometimes God's people get depressed. Remember that bad things do happen to good people, God's people. I can't answer the whys, but I can testify that he is faithful, in his time, to rescue us (Psalm 35:9 and 40:1-3).

Where does anti-depressant medication fit into this picture? Is it a cop out? Is it failing to trust in God? Let me ask, would you take antibiotics for an infection? Would you take insulin if you were diabetic? Would you take radiation or chemotherapy if it were recommended to fight your cancer? If the doctor prescribed an inhaler for your severe asthma, would you take it the next time you had an attack? Depression is often due to a chemical imbalance in the brain. Statistics show that in excess of thirty million people in America are affected by depression. For some unsubstantiated reason, many people fail to believe that it is real illness. They believe that you could just snap out of it if you had more faith, or prayed more, or confessed unforgiven sin, and a host of other things. While I certainly do not minimize the importance of dealing with these issues, they're often not the "fix all" for depression. Nowhere in the Bible can I find that it is against Christian teachings to take anti-depressant medication while under the care of a medical doctor. The medication is often the boost needed to get us over the hump to where we can rationally process information and get back on the road to recovery.

✦ "So Peter went over the side of the boat and walked on the water toward Jesus. But when he looked around at the high waives, he was terrified and began to sink. 'Save me, Lord,' he shouted. Instantly, Jesus reached out his hand and grabbed him." –Matthew 14:29-31

Larry Burkett, *Damaged But Not Broken*, Moody Press, Chicago, IL, 1996, p116.
Sheila Walsh, *Honestly*, Zondervan Publishing House, Grand Rapids, MI, 1996, p53.

HOW DO THEY DO THAT?

Years ago it was a big mystery, but today there are almost no limits to what special effects can do for television and movie drama. I remember touring part of a recording studio. We were actually able to observe a war ship, about the size of a person, get shot at by low flying aircraft, equally small in size. But boy, did it look real on the screen! For the final tour event, we watched a replica of a tug boat being tossed out of control on the high seas of a junior Olympic-size swimming pool. I'm talking things went from totally calm to hurricane status with the touch of a button or two.

Mark, Chapter 4, speaks of such a storm on the Sea of Galilee. The Sea of Galilee sits 680 feet below sea level, in the midst of numerous hills. The winds that blow over the hills intensify as they near the sea, causing violent storms to come from seemingly nowhere. Remember, the disciples had spent their lives on this lake—but they panicked on this one.

Have you ever been blind-sided by a storm of life that came out of nowhere? You know, one of those gale-forced storms with the potential of devastating you?

Let's focus on the Mark 4 film. The disciples had been around Jesus. They knew what he was about. This particular trip was his idea. I had not realized before that Jesus was such a heavy sleeper! I mean, the boat is pounding against the waves and is almost full of water (not a good sign!) and Jesus is in the back, asleep, with his head on a cushion. The disciples were frantic. They woke him by shouting at him. (Did you ever yell at anybody because you were uptight and stressed out?) "Quiet down!" he said. "Suddenly the wind stopped, and there was a great calm" (Mark 4:39). And we think voice-activated computers, special effects, and technology are so neat, Jesus did it some time around 20A.D..

Jesus has been faithful to meet the needs of his people for thousands of years, yet we, too, doubt him in the midst of our crises. The Life Application Bible scholars point out that at the time, the disciples had not yet learned enough about Jesus, but we cannot use the same excuse.

So Jesus was never diagnosed with a life-threatening disease. He was never laid off because the company was downsizing. He never had marital problems. But he was falsely accused, mocked, spat upon, beaten, and left to die on a cross. I believe he can relate!

- ✧ "And he asked them, 'Why are you so afraid? Do you still not have faith in me?'" -Mark 4:40

Life Application Bible, NIV, Tyndale House Publishers, Inc., 1991.

SOMETIMES IT FLIES, SOMETIMES IT STANDS STILL

Time stands still, that is.

The majority of those who have endured chemotherapy will confirm that when the nurses tell you that your hair is going to fall out in fourteen days, you'd better get ready. They mean business.

People commented to me about how quickly the 6 months of chemo had passed. I wanted to ask whose clock and calendar they were using because mine seemed to stand still.

For little kids, the first 24 days of December pass ever so slowly. Yet the same 24 days fly by for the parents who haven't finished their shopping.

Sometimes it flies; sometimes it seemingly stands still.

Can we stop time? It happened once, a very long time ago. God granted Joshua's request for the sun to stand still so that the Israelite army could defeat the Amorites (Joshua 10:12-14). It hasn't happened since, so Father Time is obviously not in the habit of pausing nature's clock.

Do you suppose we could delay time? I recall that King Hezekiah became deathly ill. In fact, Isaiah, the prophet, relayed a message from God. You'd better get your things in order, "for you are going to die." Naturally, Hezekiah was more than a little upset. He prayed intently. He wept bitterly. And God changed the plan. He added 5,475 days—fifteen years—to Hezekiah's life.

Short of a miracle, is there anything we can do about time? Oh, yes! Prioritize your life: God first, family second, and work third. Then order your priorities. You see, there is a difference in what is urgent and what is important.

How many times have you sat down to have dinner (it's supper here in the south) and the phone interrupted your meal? Or your cell phone rang while watching your child's ball game and you missed the one time s/he made a great play. You're in the midst of your quiet time (Bible study and prayer) and the phone rings, or the dryer cuts off, or the computer signals that you've just received an email. You've got the point. We have more conveniences—fast foods, microwaveable things, and high-tech gadgets and gizmos than at any other time in history. Yet with all of these time-saving devices, we are busier than ever before.

God had notified me, and confirmed his notification, that I was to write devotionals. You *know* what happened. I never found the time. But while recuperating from surgery and six months of chemotherapy, I had time. Boy, did I have time. I'm not at all saying that God struck me with cancer. I am saying that he was well aware that I had it. He saw me through every step of it. And he used my experience to help others. Would I want to go through it again? ABSOLUTELY NOT! On the other hand, the experience has caused me to see and experience life differently. And for that, I am grateful.

There is a time for everything (Ecclesiastes 3).

How do we set priorities? Simply give it to God.

<<<<<<<<<<◇>>>>>>>>>>

✧ "Trust in the Lord with all you heart; do not depend on your own understanding. Seek his will in all you do, and he will direct your paths." -Proverbs 3:5-6

THAT IS SO — GOD!

I was listening to Christmas music to ease the drudgery of cleaning up the kitchen when my dishwashing was interrupted by three thumps against the back side of the house, two in rapid succession and the third, not far behind. Because it had happened so many times before, I knew immediately that three birds had attempted to fly through the darkness of what they found to be a window. I dried my hands and went to see if I could render aid in the form of keeping our St. Bernard from crushing them. Each appeared to be panting (if birds pant) and was in a dazed state that obviously indicated he was seeing stars. I couldn't help but recall Jesus' words, "Not even a sparrow, worth only half a penny, can fall to the ground without the Father knowing it...You are more valuable to him than a whole flock of sparrows" (Matthew 10:29-30). I could just picture the Father fully aware, caring and compassionate. I immediately thought about the fact that I was undergoing chemotherapy. As I stood over God's tiny, helpless creatures, I realized that he cares deeply about my emotional, spiritual, and physical health. The Greek word for care is *merimma*. It refers to being so concerned that one becomes anxious and worries, not that the Father worries, but he was telling the story in a way that his listeners could understand. He is compassionate, meaning merciful and suffering with another. I am so blessed to have a friend who has been faithful to call me almost daily, and on occasion, several times in the same day just to check on me and to attend to my needs during the course of the chemo. She has prayed with me, over me, and for me. She walked the floor while I was in surgery. And she cried with me when we learned that I had cancer. But just imagine! My heavenly Father is infinitely more caring and compassionate about me! (and you!). Honestly, it is difficult to imagine. But that is so God!

I LIED TO THE MAN!

I didn't mean to. He set me up.

The doctor (radiologist) via sonogram determined that I had two tumors, and there was a good chance they were cancerous. In the next breath he asked, "How old are you?" I told him I was thirty eight. I knew immediately that I had not been thirty eight in several years. "That's not right," I told him, "but I can't tell you how old I am." Not that I was so vain, it was just that his announcement was so horrific that it had short circuited my thought process. I couldn't remember how old I was! I was not expecting his finding. I had no support team with me. I had not felt it necessary because my physician had thought the lump to be a fatty tumor.

How quickly life can change—but how faithful God will be. Mary wasn't planning on becoming pregnant before she married Joseph. Joseph didn't foresee the turn of events for his life, either. Both were afraid and initially confused about what to do. Yet they knew enough about God to trust his messenger, the angel. And aren't we glad they did!

I once read a bumper sticker that said "LIFE HAPPENS." And change is inevitable. God, in his infinite wisdom, inspired writers of the New Testament to help us deal with change by reminding us that he is always the same (Hebrews 1:12). He "is the same yesterday, today, and forever" (Hebrews 13:8). Though we may not see it, "God causes everything (not some things) to work together for the good of those that love him and are called according to his purpose for them" (Romans 8:28).

That is not to say that all things are good. But God can take what seems hopeless (at least, very unpleasant) circumstances and use them to bless us—to reveal more of his love to us, to get us from point A to point B where otherwise, we would not have gone. Remember the big picture. Life is not about God making happy campers out of all of us. Rather, we are on this earth to fulfill his plan to further his kingdom—to witness, minister to (meet the needs) of Christian brothers and sisters, to be like Christ through our adversities in order to be an example for the world. Notice the final words of Romans 8:28, "for the good of those who love God and are called according to his purpose." In other words, this verse doesn't apply to everyone—only those who have said "yes" to the Holy Spirit's invitation by asking Jesus Christ into their lives. Only then can we be sure that everything that happens in our lives is for our good. Why? Because God only wants what is best for his children. It has been said that God loves us too much to leave us the way we are.

Thankfully, God doesn't get shaken by change like I did with the radiologist. He is **always the same**.

✧ "And we know that God causes everything to work together for the good of those who love God and are called according to his purpose for them. For God knew his people in advance, and he chose them to become like his son." –Romans 8:28-29(a)

I'M SORRY, GOD

I was relaxing in the bathtub, listening to Chonda Pierce sing "Potter's Hand.

"Break me, mold me,
Use me, fill me
I give my life to the potter's hand."

But I was thinking, "God, just leave me alone!" I was half-way through my regimen of chemo. I was tired of not feeling well. I was anxious. Depressed. If this is what was meant by "break me, mold me," I wasn't sure I wanted to continue to participate. Quite frankly, I saw God's hand at work in the manner and stage in which my cancer was discovered, but I was unable to see him at the time.

I immediately apologized to God for my mental outburst. I felt compelled to go back and listen to the first part of the song.

"Beautiful Lord, Wonderful Savior,
I know for sure all of my days are held in your
hand.
Crafted into your perfect plan.
You gently call me into your presence,
Guiding me by your Holy Spirit.
Teach me, dear Lord, to live all of my life in
your eyes.
I'm captured by your holy calling,
Set me apart.

*I know you're drawing me to yourself.
Lead me Lord, I pray."*

And then I prayed, "Oh, Father, I don't want to feel like I'm wandering alone in the desert. I know you're here with me. I know that when I can't see your hand, I have got to trust your heart. I know that you are using this experienced to draw 'me to yourself.' Let me feel you and see you anew."

✧ "Yet, O Lord, you are our Father. We are the clay, and you are the potter. We are formed by your hand." –Isaiah 64:8

Potter's Hand, 1997, Darlene Zschech, Hillsongs Australia (adm. in the U.S. and Canada by Integrity's Hosanna Music, ASCAP.
Yes, & Amen, 1999, Chonda Pierce, Word Entertainment, a division of Word Music Group, Inc., 25 Music Square West Nashville, TN 37203

WHY DIDN'T YOU ANSWER, LORD?

Father, where have you been? I searched everywhere for you but couldn't sense your presence. I have read the Bible. I have prayed. You were with those people when they wandered in the wilderness for forty years. You were in the fiery furnace with those three guys—and, with Daniel in the lion's den. But, when I needed you—oh, I see the pattern. My need wasn't nearly as big of an issue as theirs. I'm sorry, God, I didn't realize—

My child, my child! Needs don't come in sizes. Each is as important to me as the other. I have been by your side every step of the way. There were times when the chemo had weakened your body so—I couldn't stand to see you stumble and fall, so I gently reached down and scooped you up in my arms and carried you for a while. Just because you can't feel my presence doesn't mean I'm not there.

Father, I need to talk to you. There is a lot about this stage of my life that I don't understand. For example, I have prayed and prayed, for years, that I would never get cancer. It was one of my biggest fears. You have the power to raise people from the dead. Some you have even taken directly to heaven without them dying. You parted the water several times to let people cross over on dry land, yet you didn't answer my prayer. Help me to understand. What did I do to cause—

Beth, do you remember when you surrendered your life to me?

Yes, Father. I had been a Christian for several years. I was at a youth camp in Minden, LA. That was almost thirty years ago.

Oh, my child, it seems just like yesterday. I was so touched that you grasped the idea of allowing me to direct your life—to carry out the master plan, to unfold the drama as I saw fit, to orchestrate the music to sooth your soul and to inspire you. I remember, you kind of took the reins in your own hands a few time, but you learned rather quickly the comfort of knowing that I was in control—that I always looked out for your best interest. You learned to turn it all over to me so you wouldn't make a mistake or have to worry about it. When you gave me control of your life, do you remember what you were thinking?

Yes, Father. You have a great big world out there with lots of people that need to know about you. They are **not yet your children**. And ***you have a lot of children*** that need help getting through the struggles of life. Some have picked up the reins, just as I did. They need to be guided back on to the right path.

You're absolutely right. My ways are not your ways. You've seen me do things so many times that were "so God," as you call them. Your whole purpose on this earth is to further my kingdom.

Father, I have heard that phrase "further (your) kingdom" all of my life. I've even used it. But, what, exactly, does it mean?

Let me explain it this way. Everyone on earth will eventually die. I have prepared an awesome place for everybody. But, not all choose to make reservations in heaven by asking me to forgive them. Not everyone is willing to give me control of their life. You, my child, are hope to a dying world. By going through the physical, mental, and spiritual agony of cancer, people were able to see how I blessed you, even in the midst of it. They saw that you were experiencing a peace that the world could not give. They saw that you were not angry at me. Had you not gone through the aftermath of cancer, you would not have been able to write devotionals that will help so many who are faced with the trials of every day life. You are my messenger. Your purpose is twofold—-to share with those that are not yet my children about why I came to live among them and then to die and what I can do for them on earth. And you have the responsibility of ministering to and mentoring some of my children. In so doing, you will help to deepen their faith and spiritual walk. In other words, you are helping me to make disciples. Do you see, my child, it's not that I didn't answer your prayer. You gave me your life to use to further my kingdom, and, in your case, the cancer ordeal has brought you to a much deeper dimension spiritually. I inspired Dr. Luke, around A.D.70 to write..."Much is required from those to whom much is given. And much more is required from those to whom much more is given" (Luke 12:48). Until I come, I am depending on you. I will give increased responsibilities and opportunities to my faithful followers. The more resources, talents, and understanding I give, the more I expect them to be used responsibly and effectively. I will not hold you accountable for the use of gifts that I have not given you. Oh, how I can bless you on earth and reward you in heaven if you remain faithful.

More than anything, when you throw open those pearly gates, Father, I want you to be able to say, "well done, good job, you helped to further my kingdom."

THE NIGHT SHOOT

Firing a weapon at a still target in the daytime is one thing, but firing at the same target at night with various intensities of strobe lights flashing around you is a horse of a different color! (Did you ever wonder how that phrase originated? At any rate, if you've been there and done that you know exactly what I mean.) My first experience with that phenomenon was in the police academy—the infamous "Night Shoot!"

At one point in my life, I was undergoing chemotherapy and attempting to deal with all of the emotional issues that go along with it. I found Stormie OMartian's book "Just Enough Light for the Step I'm On" to be particularly relevant. She posed the question, "Why can't I have all the light I need right now, Lord," in an effort to make some rhyme or reason to the downhill turn in life's events. She explained that "God knows that too much light can be hard to take. It can blind and confuse us." I know that's right! My thoughts immediately went back to the "Night Shoot." As rookies, we couldn't imagine that shooting in the dark could be all that difficult. How could it be with headlights of police units (cruisers, for some of you), spot lights, and red, blue, and amber visibar lights to illuminate our targets? The truth is, they distorted our view, big time! In the midst of my chemo experience, God allowed me to reflect on the "Night Shoot" to show me that it really was not important that I understand why me, why cancer, why that particular time, but my response to God's direction after the chemo was the paramount issue.

Consider this: Had God shed enough light for Jonah to see that he would be swallowed by a big fish, don't you think he would have scrambled to find the off switch? I don't think Daniel would've been elated if God had shed light on the fact that he would be a lion tamer, either. The Bible is replete with such examples.

I thank God that, in his infinite wisdom, he kept the fact that I would have to battle cancer at age 43 — until I turned 43.

"For I know the plans that I have for you, says the Lord," (Jeremiah 29:11 NLT). I find it is best when I leave the master plan to the Master. He need only give me directions one day at a time. Remember, he didn't promise that we would have no pain, suffering, hardships, or adversities. But he did promise to see us through to a triumphant finish!

- ✧ "For I know the plans I have for you," says the Lord. "They are plans for good and not for disaster, to give you a future and a hope. In those days when you pray, I will listen. If you look for me in earnest, you will find me when you seek me." – Jeremiah 29:11-13

Stormie Omartian, *Just Enough Light for the Step I'm On-Trusting God in the Tough Times,"* Harvest House Publishers, Eugene, Oregon 97402, 1999.

IT CAN SOOTHE THE SOUL

Or, it can make you a nervous wreck! Music, that is.

I am from a family that loves music and I married into a family that loves it. We would sing and harmonize while traveling down the road. If we were camping, gathering around the camp fire with our guitars was a given. The guitars are still very much a part of our family reunions. I have been involved in church and city musical productions all of my life. I like a wide variety of music, but there are some types that "rev-up" my stress level. For example, rap is not my favorite thing, nor is bluegrass. I can do without opera. Heavy metal is definitely not my thing. And I'm not fond of the cheatin', lyin', s/he's run off, cryin' and slingin' snot songs either.

In one of the criminal justice courses that I teach, we discuss some of the unique sentences that judges have handed down to various law breakers. It seems as though there were some teenage boys that loved music. They loved it so much that they wanted to share it with everyone in their city. Not only could citizens within a city block hear it loud and clear, but they could feel it, deep within the depths of their souls, if you know what I mean. It definitely registered on the upper level of the decibel meter. The boys were ticketed. The judge was creative and thoughtful enough to give them, and those who followed in their footsteps, a sentence they would remember. They were mandated to report for the biggest part of two days to a location where they were supervised. The judge, out of the goodness of his heart, allowed them to listen to music while they did their time. Whatever types of music they despised, the judge "allowed" them to listen to —loud and without ceasing. What a brilliant sentence!

During my cancer and chemo ordeal, the American Cancer Society's *Look Good, Feel Better* program emphasized that there would be days that we wouldn't feel like getting up much less getting dressed. But they urged us to do it anyway, because when you look good, you feel better.

Even though I was out of bed and dressed but on the couch, on occasion I was emotionally down. I began to realize that on those days, I could control the situation, somewhat, with music. Slower music dragged me down. It was depressing. (Yes, I like slow songs, but they don't mix with depression.) I learned to positively influence my emotions by listening to something a little more upbeat. Contemporary Christian music was often my choice. Not only was it upbeat, but it kept me in touch with God—and hope.

The same holds true for mega situations in every day life. So get out the good music. Throw back the curtains and let the sun shine in. Turn on the lights. Brighten up the place. You might just get caught up in it. You can make b-e-a-u-t-i-f-u-l music or you can make a joyful noise. God's not picky about his music.

- "David assigned men to lead the music. They ministered with music." –I Chronicles 6:31-32
- "Then I will hold my head high, above my enemies who surround me, singing and praising the Lord with music." –Psalm 27:6
- "Don't act thoughtlessly, but try to understand what the Lord wants you to do. Don't be drunk with wine, because that will ruin your life. Instead, let the Holy Spirit fill and control you. Then you will sing psalms and hymns and spiritual songs among yourselves, making music to the Lord in your hearts. And you will always give thanks for everything to God the Father in the name of our Lord Jesus Christ." -Ephesians 5: 17-20.

A CALMNESS THAT IS BEYOND HUMAN COMPREHENSION

With all of the bad that is happening around me, I should be screaming! I should be angry! I could be filled with hatred. I should be crying without stopping. I do cry some briefly. But I have an overall peace that sometimes even I don't understand. Granted, when first diagnosed with cancer, my days and nights were filled with worry—not the kind that moves to an appropriate action, but the inappropriate kind that strikes fear and depression.

Worry or concern is a natural part of life. We do it all the time. They did it in A.D. 61 when Paul penned Philippians from his jail cell in Rome. But too much worry about things that we have no control over is not a good thing. Worry and anxiety are detrimental to good health. There is not much positive about it. It can consume your thoughts. One who worries excessively is unable to accomplish much. One who worries is really not trusting God with the issues.

Paul said in Philippians 4:7, "Don't worry about anything, instead pray about everything. Tell God what you need, and thank him for all he has done. If you do this, you will experience God's peace which is far more wonderful than the human mind can understand." Jesus, himself said "Can all your worries add a single moment to your life? Of course not" (Matthew 6:27). In fact, it will likely take a few years off it.

Paul's answer to worry was prayer. If you want to worry less, then pray more! Positive and negative thoughts cannot occupy the human mind at the same time—so quote scripture, sing praise and worship songs, pray out loud—leave no room for worry to filter in. I once received advice from a mentor. He said, "Ask yourself, what is the worst possible thing that could happen in this situation? Once you've identified it, ask yourself how you would deal with that worse case scenario. When you know that you could deal with the worst, then forget it and start living." Remember, you're not in your dilemma alone. There are friends and relatives, and your heavenly Father will never leave you hanging.

It's about letting go and gaining control at the same time. Peace is the invisible glue that holds our emotions together when they ought to be falling apart. The key to that indescribable kind of peace is to give at all to God—and don't turn around and pick anything back up.

- "Give all your worries and cares to God, for he cares about you." -1 Peter 5:7
- "God, the one and only—I'll wait as long as he says. Everything I hope for comes from him, so why not? He's solid rock under my feet, breathing room for my soul, an impregnable castle: I'm set for life. My help and glory are in God—granite-strength and safe-harbor-God—So trust him absolutely, people; lay

your lives on the line for him. God is a safe place to be. –Psalm 62:5-8 (*The Message*)

THAT'S NOT ME IN THE MIRROR

That's my body, but there are so many scars, extra parts, and parts missing. Give me a little while and I'll dress it up to where no one will know. Yes, I cried at the sight a number of times until I came to realize that's not me in the mirror. I'm still a wife and a mother. I'm a sister and a friend. I'm a teacher and a student. I'm a child and an adult. I'm a committee member and I'm a fan in the stands. I'm a choir member. I am a whole lot of things to a whole lot of people. What I look like is not nearly as important as who I am—my personality, my character traits—the qualities that make me, ME!

Shortly after I lost all of my hair from chemo, a Federal Express truck pulled into my driveway. I knew I had not ordered anything. Yet there was a man at my door with a large box bearing my name. Naturally, I tore into the unexpected package and much to my surprise, there were 19 hats, each eagerly awaiting its turn on my bald head. Some demanded a laugh. Some were dressy, others were casual, and a few were downright hideous. But they were special. Maybe it would be more correct to say each had character. I called the person whose name appeared on the return address. Donna was quiet initially, awaiting my reaction. She knew it would either make me mad or make me laugh. She hoped for the latter—and it worked! For a period of time, she took my mind off of me. What a brilliant expression of love, acceptance, empathy, and friendship. She was pulling for me in my time of loss and depression.

I'll admit. I found the loss of my hair to be much more devastating than the surgeries that caused all of the scars and missing and extra parts. It's not that I'm vain, but hair loss is often a very emotional thing, especially for women. How did I deal with it? You won't believe. I shaved my head! Yes, you read it correctly. I SHAVED MY HEAD! Actually, a cosmetologist who volunteers for the "Look Good, Feel Better" program did it, free of charge. Why? Because when your hair begins to fall out, it does it in a big way. When the inevitable begins, you can have control over the situation. Shave it and put on your wig. (Need I say that it is recommended that you purchase and style your wig BEFORE shaving your head?!) I remember the day: I was literally afraid that my hair would be gone with the wind before I could get to my "hair" appointment.

"Look Good, Feel Better" is a wonderful service for Oncology patients. It is a community service of the American Cancer Society in hospitals in many cities. The purpose is to educate the patient. I mean, if your hair fell out would you know how far down to place a wig on your forehead? I don't think so. If you lost your eyebrows, would you have any idea of where to draw them and how to make them look natural? Of course not. And do you know the secrets of buying and putting on false eyelashes? Now that's a real trip! Do they have a left and a right? (We're not used to taking off our eyelashes before going to bed or taking a shower. I'm telling you, if they are not yours, you'd better take them off or you'll end up with them in some strange places!) When you look good, you feel better—really!

If you want my opinion (you're getting it anyway), be honest with people. The majority of people who undergo chemo loose their hair. What's the big deal about telling people, "I lost my hair?" (I don't mean broadcast it. I mean tell your circle of friends.) The big deal is that you'll have people to encourage you. They won't have to worry about offending you. You can divide your grief and multiply your joy because you'll have somebody to cry WITH you and laugh WITH you.

Case in point. It was New Years 2000. Fireworks are an essential part of the celebration. Do you have any idea what damage sparks do to store-bought synthetic hair? Inevitably, someone will ignite an entire package of firecrackers or turn the Roman Cannon the wrong way, sending everyone scurrying, and you have to beat your head to keep from melting your hair. It can be emotionally painful, or you can laugh about it. I chose to laugh. Laughter is medicinal, you know. (A cheerful heart is good medicine, but a broken spirit saps a person's strength" Proverbs 17:22.) And then there was the time that my eyelash came loose at the family reunion. But I lived to laugh about it.

My family loves me with or without hair. My dog and cat don't know the difference. My relationships with my friends remain unchanged. And my heavenly Father hears my voice and knows that I am his. He isn't bothered by my changed appearance.

<<<<<<<<<<◇>>>>>>>>>>

- ✧ "Don't be concerned about the outward beauty that depends on fancy hairstyles, expensive jewelry, or beautiful clothes. You should be known for the beauty that comes from within, the unfading beauty of a gentle and quiet spirit, which is so precious to God." -1 Peter 3:3-5
- ✧ "Don't judge by his appearance or height, for I have rejected him. The Lord doesn't make decision the way you do. People judge by outward appearance, but the Lord looks at a person's thoughts and intentions." -1 Samuel 16:7

I THOUGHT THAT VERSE WAS RESERVED FOR FUNERALS

At least that's the only place I have ever heard it! Well, maybe in a few sermons. "Let not your heart be troubled. Ye believe in God, believe also in me. I go to prepare a place for you" (John 14:27 KJV). Most of us are familiar with this verse. It promises a place to us in our hereafter. But what does it do for us today? A lot! When Jesus was explaining the role of the Holy Spirit, he said "I am leaving you with a gift: peace of mind and peace of heart. And the peace I give isn't like the peace the world gives. So don't be troubled or afraid" (John 12:27). That is totally awesome! Peace! No trouble! No fear! How is that possible?

When my daughter was preparing for an overseas mission trip to a third world country, she was told repeatedly "there is no safer place than in the center of God's will." When my life is spinning hopelessly out of control, only when I step away from the control panel, can God restore me. He is not going to push past me or grab me and shove me out of his way. He will never regain control by force, only by submission. Then I can find peace in the center of his will.

"And the peace I give you isn't like the peace the world gives." Thank goodness! Our daily news is filled with accounts in which the individual was peaceful one minute and violently out of control the next. Many countries are peaceful today and at war tomorrow. Our Father's peace is solid! It is real! It is deep! It is dependable! It is forever!

Every time I have found myself in a situation that I certainly would not have chosen, one in which I have little or no control over it's outcome, I have come to the conclusion that I would rather be in the midst of that situation, in all of its awfulness, if that is where God wanted me at the time. To be out of God's will for my life would mean not walking with him, not talking to him, nor having his guidance on a daily basis. That would be sheer misery for me — much worse than the awful situation. David wrote of such agony. He said, "Do not banish me from your presence and don't take your Holy Spirit from me" (Psalm 51:11).

So don't be troubled or afraid. "I am leaving you a gift of peace of mind and heart" (John 14:27).

✧ "And do not bring sorrow to God's Holy Spirit by the way you live. Remember, he is the one who had identified you as his own." –Ephesians 4:30

GOD DOESN'T DEAL IN PERCENTAGES

But if he did, the Bible might read something like this:

* 14% of each week shall be allocated to rest
* 100% of Pharaoh's army perished beneath the waves of the Red Sea
* 91.7% of Jesus' original disciples were good guys (Judas was the only really bad one)
* .02% of the crowd that gathered to hear Jesus speak near Bethsaida brought food (1 out of approximately 5000 brought 5 loaves and 2 fishes)
* 86% of the disciples Jesus chose returned from the towns and villages; of those, 100% reported that even the demons obeyed when they used Jesus' name (Luke 10:1)
* God does not want any (0%) to live in hell forever. He wants everyone (100%) to live with him in heaven forever.

But the Bible doesn't read that like that. God doesn't deal in percentages.

When I first learned that I had cancer, I began to gather information to broaden my knowledge about the disease. Friends brought books and referred me to websites. My mom dog-eared lots of magazine articles that related to the subject. The bottom line was that I was much more confused and distraught than before I began my research. Why? Because there is so much contradictory information. One source suggested that I eat certain preventive foods. Some articles suggested that some earlier studies were not as valid as once thought. Some recommended certain vitamin and/or food supplements. Others said that's good if you have this type of cancer, but if you have that kind of cancer it can worsen your condition. My patient education nurse informed me that 80% of the patients on a certain type of chemo medication lose their hair. I was in that 80%. When I read the patient information on the preventive drug I would be taking for five years, there were all kinds of horrifying stats about various side effects. The question was do I take the medication to prevent one type of cancer but risk it causing another type of cancer? Wonderful odds! So what's a person to do? I chose to quit reading all of the stuff that was upsetting me. I put my faith and trust in my God and in my Christian oncologist, who consults with the Great Physician on each of his patient treatment plans. (I never wanted my own personal oncologist, but I'm sure glad I've got the one I do!)

It boils down to this: I don't want to know the odds of a recurrence. God doesn't deal in percentages. Well, maybe he does. He said, "I will never leave you or forsake you" (Hebrews 13:5). I think that can be interpreted to mean that he is with me and in control 100% of the time. My God doesn't make mistakes. So it is up to me to submit, to willfully give, my life to him so that he can use every aspect of it for his glory—meaning, to give him the honor and the attention that he deserves.

FACTS VERSUS FEELINGS

I can't be sick! I don't look sick. And I certainly don't feel sick. (That is, until I started chemo.) But what I felt like did not change the circumstances one bit. I still had cancer.

The Christian life can be a lot like that. I don't feel forgiven. I don't feel worthy of my Father's grace and salvation. I don't feel like my prayers are heard. And I don't feel like God really cares or he wouldn't have allowed this to happen. But the facts remain: God does care. We can be truly forgiven. And he does hear and answer our prayers.

- ✧ "Give all of your worries and cares to God, for he cares about what happens to you." -1 Peter 5:7
- ✧ "Therefore, he is able, once and forever, to save everyone who comes to God through him. He lives forever to plead with God on their behalf." –Hebrews 7:25

I USED TO RAISE MY EYEBROWS, TOO

And then I didn't have an eyebrow to raise. Chemo claimed them.

Have you ever seen a female with super short hair, maybe spiked up a bit? Come on. Admit it. You probably gave her the once over, raised your eyebrows, and commented to yourself—weird, strange, unique, or some equally descriptive verb. I've done the same thing, but now I look at them and wonder if they are just getting over chemo. Remember the old adage, "You can't tell a book by its cover?" I mean, the middle aged lady that's too old to wear her hair like **that** just may not have a choice. Or maybe she's found her free spirit, like the members of the *Red Hat Society*! Go girls!

Speaking of choices! When we find ourselves in a Job-like situation we can either curse God and die, as was suggested to Job, or we can choose to hold tightly to his hand and allow him to lead us through the muck of the horrible situation. Suffering can be but isn't always a penalty for sin. By the same token, prosperity is not a sure sign of being rewarded for being good. God's children simply are not exempt from trouble. Although we may not be able to fully understand the pain that we experience it can lead us to a closer relationship with our heavenly Father. We have to learn to recognize the devil's attacks and cling to the knowledge that Satan cannot do as he pleases. He cannot go beyond the limits that God sets for him. It is of utmost importance that we not allow any adverse situation or experience to drive a wedge between ourselves and our heavenly Father. We may not be able to choose what will happen to us (I'm not sure I would want to anyway) but we can always choose how we will respond when "it" happens.

✧ "Then choose today whom you will serve. But as for me and my family, we will serve the Lord." –Joshua24:15 (The Message)

HOW NOT TO BE EATEN BY A LION

Front and center. That's where I found myself in my thoughts. I was worried about whether cancer would come back. What people thought about my store-bought hair and eye lashes bothered me. The possibility of catching the flu or a virus while my immune system was down from chemo concerned me. How much work would I miss? And sometimes, I just outright had a pity party! All of these things and much more occupied my mind. It kept me anxious, discouraged, and depressed. I realized that I was too focused on **me** and not focused enough on God. I needed for him to rescue me from myself. The fact is, we can be our own worst enemy.

It's not a new idea. Peter (1 Peter 5:8-9) cautioned believers to "Be careful! Watch out for attacks from the Devil, your great enemy. He prowls around like a roaring lion, looking for some victim to devour. Take a firm stand against him, and be strong in your faith. Remember that your Christian brothers and sisters all over the world are going through the same kind of suffering you are." Not necessarily physical suffering, but mental anguish of varying degrees.

We've all seen shows on television of African lions stalking wounded or weaker animals for their next meal. Or they may pick on the ones that aren't alert—the ones that stand around daydreaming. We can have oodles of friends around us, but when we get down, we feel so alone. We barely have enough energy to get through life. We feel helpless. That makes us potential lion food! In order not to be eaten by a lion, we have to focus on the Master lion tamer—Jesus Christ! Then, "he (Satan) will flee from you" (James 4:7).

When Johoshaphat was King of Judah he received news that a very large army was moving in to attack. The people had built a temple. When faced with any calamity such as war, disease, or famine, they would gather in the temple courtyard. "We cry out to you to save us, and you will hear us and rescue us." Johoshaphat was in the process of telling God, out loud, how serious the impending situation looked when "the Spirit of the Lord" came to Jahaziel, one of the men in the crowd. Jahaziel informed the people that they didn't have to worry at all "for the battle is not yours, but God's" (2 Chronicles 20:15).

So it is with us. We battle so many emotions: anger, depression, defeat, and the list goes on. This is the way Satan lures us away so he can devour us. As children of God, the Holy Spirit is in each of us. We are so human; he is so Divine. His ways are not our ways. We must be careful to seek after God's interests rather than our own. Then he will fight our daily battles for us. And he won't allow us to be lion food.

<<<<<<<<<<◇>>>>>>>>>>

-  "Tomorrow, march out against them. But, you will not even need to fight. Take your positions, then stand still and watch the Lord's victory. He is with you…Do not be afraid or discouraged. Go out there tomorrow, for the Lord is with you." -2 Chronicles 20:17

SPIRITUAL TIME OUT

Time Out for corrective behavior was not a part of my childhood. Oh, I was disciplined alright, but it was much more severe than spending time alone thinking about the error of my ways. So I never experienced time out until God put me there, or at least he allowed me to experience what I call "spiritual time out." Remember Jonah? God put him in time out in the belly of a whale (okay, fish, if you must!). I'll be the first to admit that spiritual time out is a phenomenon I don't fully understand. In fact, I'm not sure I even begin to understand. But it is real. Others have shared their experiences with me. As best I can tell, it comes on the heels of a traumatic event.

What happens during spiritual time out? At first I described it as being numb, but with numbness you don't feel anything. I felt very much alone, though I was in contact with numerous people each day. I experienced fear, anxiety, and an emptiness, as if something had been taken from me. I had tons of head knowledge about God and his promise never to leave me or forget me. After all, I am a P.K. (preacher's kid!)! But, for several months I couldn't see him. I couldn't feel him. Studying the Bible was no more than words on a page—head knowledge. Singing praise and worship songs was just musical notes lingering in the air. There was no emotion behind them. I can best explain it by using the analogy of a picture that has been around for years. Remember the one with the little girl standing in the corner with her face toward the wall? Her puppy sits waiting patiently beside her, though she can't see him. I knew God was there, but I couldn't feel him or see him. Why not? I have no clue! Maybe that's what it took to get my attention. Maybe God allows us to go through spiritual time out as a coping mechanism. I do know that traumatic experiences tend to make us take a spiritual inventory. It is easy during those times to allow questions, fears, and doubts to overcome us.

I was not angry at God. I was not asking, "why **me**?" I did wonder why and what I was to do or learn as a result of the cancer experience. I even asked God to help me get it right the first time so I wouldn't have to go through it again!

Once you have experienced God—I mean really experienced God—felt his presence, depended on his daily guidance through the Holy Spirit—spiritual time out is awful! My advice: keep going through the motions. Joy comes in the morning.

✧ "Weeping may go on all night but joy comes with the morning." –Psalm 30:5(b)

PUT YOUR FEET IN FIRST

A lot of what God says he will do for us is conditional. I'm not sure if we just skip over that part of the scripture accidentally while focusing on his promises, or if we willfully choose not to pay attention to it.

Referring to Joshua, Chapter 3 it seems as though the Israelites needed God's help to cross over the water again. You will recall that after being slaves for 400 years, Moses led them out of Egypt. God had parted the Red Sea to get them out and now they needed to cross over the Jordan River to get in to Canaan, the Promised Land. In order to cross the Jordan, God had given strict instructions that their priests must first step into the water. Bear in mind, they were carrying the Ark of the Covenant of the Lord, the object that was the most sacred to them.

Time out for a brief history reminder: the ark looked like a wooden box, about 45" long, 27" wide, and 27" high. Poles were inserted into rings on the long side of the box so that it could be carried by four men. The lid was covered in gold. Two carved cherubim (winged creatures) sat on top. The Ark contained the two stone tablets on which God had written the Ten Commandments and then gave to Moses. It housed Aaron's staff and contained two quarts of manna. Each was a reminder that God had provided for their needs for the entire forty years that they had wandered in the wilderness. The Israelites believed that God lived among them between the wings of the two cherubim which were mounted on the gold lid. In fact, when Moses was in the Tabernacle (Numbers 7:8-9), he heard the voice of God come from that very place—the place of atonement, which symbolizes the act of God that covers our sin. The purpose of the Tabernacle was so that the people could have a tangible place to experience the presence of God. It was a Holy Place. Men, seventy of them, would later die because they looked into the Ark with irreverent curiosity (1 Samuel 6:19). And David would mobilize thirty thousand special troops to bring home the Ark. They would transport it incorrectly. The oxen would stumble and Uzzah would reach out to steady the Ark. Wrong move! God would strike him dead because he had given specific instruction that the Ark was only to be carried by the Levites (priests) and even they were never to touch the Ark. To touch it, under Hebrew law, was a capital offense. God was serious about his people following his instructions.

Back to the instructions: In order to cross the river, the priests had to take a few steps into the Jordan River and stand there. What if they had said, "I don't think so." After all, it was spring. The water could have been rather chilly. Do you realize that over two million people needed to cross over? Can you imagine how long the priests would have to stand in the river bed for two million people to pass them? What if their priestly intuition caused them to have visions of what would happen to Uzzah? The river was at flood stage. They didn't know how deep the water was. What if one of the four priests stepped in a hole and the other three reached out to steady the Ark? Not a good scene. The bottom line is that because the priests did as they were instructed by Joshua, the river separated, and all two million walked across on dry ground. God was with them on the final leg of their journey just as he had been in the beginning.

We all come to rivers in our lives—obstacles—things that prevent us from moving forward. Some of them are real—tangible. Others serve as excuses. Some we can build a bridge and get over. Others leave us standing at the edge of the water, staring at the other side. Sometimes he leads us beside peaceful streams so he can renew our strength (Psalm 23). Quite frequently, God will not provide any solutions until we first step into the water, when we trust him, and act in obedience to what we know he wants us to do. As we are **doing**, he provides solutions—some that we never dreamed possible.

What happens when we find ourselves in **deep water**? For some reason, I saved a page off a daily tear-off calendar from 1997. It said, "A good thought to remember is, 'God brings men into deep waters, not to drown them, but to cleanse them.' You're not drowning, you are being cleansed. So hold on—and don't give up!" While that may hold true some of the time, it is not the case all of the time. Sometimes he leads us into the water, through valleys and up mountains so that we can learn to be totally dependant on him. It doesn't necessarily result from sin, though sometimes it does. Now and then, God uses these obstacles to change our direction. Even then, it doesn't mean that we were going the wrong direction. It is only after we step into the water that he gives us the life raft. He has to see the commitment first.

If you find yourself treading water, take a spiritual inventory. Ask God to show you anything in your life that is displeasing to him. Ask for his forgiveness for each specific area. Find a time every day to spend alone with God for Bible Study and prayer. You'll be amazed at how God, through the Holy Spirit, impresses upon you his directions for your life.

Oh, remember to put your feet in first. He'll reach out and take your hand and lead you.

- ✧ "Without wavering, let us hold tightly to the hope (faith) we say we have, for God can be trusted to keep his promise." –Hebrew 10:23
- ✧ "It was by faith that Abraham obeyed when God called him...he went without knowing where he was going." -Hebrews 11:8

AND GOD SAID, "WHAT DID THE DOCTOR DIAGNOSE?"

Allow me to point out a few **questionable quotes** from God.

Isaiah 6:8 records the Lord asking, "Whom should I send as a messenger to my people? Who will go for us? And, of course, Isaiah said, 'Lord, I'll go! Send me.' " (Like God didn't know?)

"The Lord God called to Adam, "Where are you?" (Genesis 3:9)

In 1 Kings 19:3, God came to Elijah in a cave. God said, "What are you doing here, Elijah?"

That is like God asking me, "What did the doctor diagnose, Beth?" I mean, HE **IS** GOD!

But these questions are nothing compared to the ones he bombarded Job with.

Check out Job 38 and 39. God asked thirty-nine rather difficult questions in Chapter 38 and he didn't let up in Chapter 39. God inquires of Job: Where is hail and rain and snow made and stored? He cross-examined Job on where light comes from and where the darkness goes each day? Can you keep the stars from moving? Can you shout to the clouds and make it rain? Who gives instinct and intuition? Job is asked to explain the size of the earth. God's line of questioning covers cosmology, geography, oceanography, and what conversation would be complete without discussing the weather? The questions move to inanimate creation to the animate. (It sort of reminds me of my worst day in court as a criminal investigator.)

So, what was God's point? He didn't ask because he didn't know! He questioned to make man think—to make him face the inner battle between the spirit and the flesh.

In 1 Kings 19, Elijah had been on the run trying to save his life. The Israelites had broken their covenant with the Lord God, torn down God's altars, and killed all of the prophets, with the exception of Elijah. Elijah was physically exhausted. God prescribed rest, food, and drink. He even sent an angel to wake him so he could eat and drink again. Elijah was feeling lonely, severely depressed, discouraged, and sorry for himself—worse than that, he was suicidal—at least he wanted God to take his life. Elijah thought he was the only one in his predicament. In a self-righteous manner, he complained about his own faithfulness. In effect, he was saying his faith didn't do him any good. "Look at the situation I am in now." God instructed the prophet to exit the cave and stand before him on the mountain. Elijah chose not to obey. A mighty windstorm hit the mountain that housed the cave, followed by an earthquake and fire, none of which phazed Elijah. But through the sound of a gentle whisper, God revealed himself and Elijah knew his voice. You see, God doesn't always reveal himself in mighty and miraculous ways. If we look for him only in big things and events, we just might miss him altogether. He is often found gently whispering in the quietness to a humbled heart.

Just as God's instruction failed to make Elijah leave the cave, Elijah's instruction failed to compel the nation of Israel to turn from their sins. Had Elijah not been so preoccupied with himself in the situation, he would have realized that there was really no difference between his heart and the hardened hearts of the Israelites.

In times of turmoil in our lives, it is so easy to get perturbed at God. We are so much like Elijah and the nation of Israel in thinking that our faithfulness has been vain because of a predicament in which we might find ourselves. Dr. Billy Graham was asked if he thought God was unfair by allowing him to have Parkinson's and other medical problems when he had served God so faithfully for so many years. Dr. Graham said," I did not see it that way at all. The key is how we react to it, either turning away from God in anger and bitterness or growing closer to him in trust and confidence."

At times, I have had to abandon my pity party, lay the blame game to rest, back away from the noise and busyness and quietly and humbly wait for God to change my attitude and ways of life. During my cancer ordeal, I finally came to a point of peace when I accepted the fact that I would rather be in God's will, even if it meant suffering and death, than to be outside of the will of my Father. I surrendered—gave up my inner fight—in order to let God be God.

Life Application Bible-NIV (Commentary), Tyndale House Publishers, Inc., Wheaton, IL 60189, 1991.

William McDonald, *Believer's Bible Commentary*, Thomas Nelson Publishers, Nashville, TN, 1995.

Home Life, LifeWay, Dr. Billy Graham, June 2000.

A FISH, A PLANT, A WORM, AND A SCORCHING WIND

The company that my husband worked for had just closed its doors but God had been faithful to provide another source of income for him. It would require moving to another city. The day we knew we would be moving the phone rang. Wouldn't you know it! The investigative position I had applied for a year earlier was now available. It was mine if I wanted it. Boy, did I want it! But I had to inform the caller that my family was moving and I would not be able to accept the position. As I hung up the phone I told God, "I really don't see the humor in this. In fact, I don't like it at all. But I have enough sense to know that you are God and you can see the big picture. So give me the patience and wisdom to follow you."

Later that evening, I shared my conversation with God with my husband. He inquired, "Aren't you afraid to talk to God like that?" I answered, "Why? He knows what I'm thinking anyway. Besides I acknowledged that he was God. I gave him his rightful place."

In one way, Jonah reminds me of me. He spoke his mind even to God. There was no holding back. Remember he was a prophet. His job description required him to be a spokesman for God. It's not like he had to prepare speeches because God put all of the words in his head. He just had to go and deliver the message. Granted, most prophets were given messages for their own people. Jonah, however, was told to go to Ninevah, the rising world power of that day. The Ninevites were hated by most everybody. They had plotted against God, exploited the helpless, were heartless conquerors in war, and practiced prostitution, witchcraft, and idol worship. Jonah had no intention of sharing the good news of God's love and mercy with them because he was afraid that they **would** repent. Strange attitude for a prophet wouldn't you say? So when Jonah received his travel itinerary to go to Ninevah, which was about 500 miles northeast of Israel, he bought a ship ticket and headed the opposite direction "hoping that by going to the west he could escape from the Lord (Jonah 1:3)." Where did he come up with that idea? "As the ship sailed along suddenly the Lord flung a powerful wind over the sea." The sailors cast lots to see who among them had offended the gods and caused the storm. When Jonah lost the toss, he finally 'fessed up. He admitted that he was running from God and the only way to save the ship was to throw him overboard. Notice that he didn't offer to jump. The hesitant sailors finally chunked him into the raging waters and begged that God not hold them accountable for his life. They did not know that God had orchestrated the entire scenario. He had even "arranged" for a great fish to swallow Jonah. You can image, Jonah had a **come to Jesus meeting** while in the belly of the whale. He had a lot of time alone with God, three days and three nights down under. I don't know if the fish was a slow swimmer, if it took the scenic route, or if it just took that long for God to get his point across to Jonah. At any rate, Jonah's prayer was one of thanksgiving, rather than deliverance (Jonah 2:1-9). He knew that he was in God's life boat. When Jonah exited his submarine, he delivered his one sentence sermon to the Ninevites. The greatest revival of all time broke out—the entire city repented. Their repentance kept God from destroying them. God's change of plans had really ticked off Jonah—so much that he prayed to die. You would think that after the big fish ordeal his attitude would have been a little different. Why was he so angry? The people were so wicked. And Jonah may have worried about his own reputation. After all, if the people repented then his own prophecy would not come true (Jonah 3:3). Jonah went outside of the city to pout. He made a shelter which God spruced up with a lovely plant. It provided him the much needed shade from the sun and even lifted his spirits somewhat, but then God sent the worm. It ate through the stem, causing the plant to die. And if that were not enough, God sent a scorching wind to really make life miserable for Jonah. Again, Jonah wanted to die. Permission was not granted. God, as a loving father, tried to reason with Jonah but the prophet's priorities were definitely not in order. He was more concerned over the dead plant than he was with 120,000 people headed directly for hell.

There is no "Plan B" with God. We can go kicking and screaming, despondent and unhappy, or we can accept the changes in life as being part of God's perfect plan, regardless. When we don't get the verdict that we feel was just, when we get passed over for promotions, when life's ups and downs are mostly down, God is still in charge. We just need to make sure that if God is trying to give us an attitude adjustment that we adjust—or risk being thrown overboard. Notice that God worked in spite of the Jonah mentality. I pray that I never push God to the point of having to gain my attention through some drastic measure.

✧ "When I had lost all hope, I turned my thoughts once more to the Lord." –Jonah 2:7

Life Application Bible-NIV (Commentary), Tyndale House Publishers, Inc., Wheaton, IL 60189, 1991.

The Open Bible, New Living Translation, Thomas Nelson, Inc., 1998.

Beth Moore, *To Live Is Christ,* LifeWay Press, Nashville, TN, 1997.

THE ISSUE WE DON'T WANT TO DISCUSS

"Even when I walk through the dark valley of death..." (Psalm 23:4). I have never liked that verse and I especially don't like it now. Coming face to face with cancer, to me, is being in the valley. That phrase has never been a comfort to me. In fact quite the contrary. I am not afraid of the hereafter. I just don't like the thought of leaving my loved ones, experiencing the physical and emotional pain of death, and there are a lot of things on earth I've not yet accomplished.

Is it okay for me to feel that way? What would Jesus think? I don't think he minds me questioning, but I do think he wants me to research it enough to come to grips with it.

You see, yesterday I attended the funeral of a very dear friend, 56 years of age. She learned that she had cancer within two weeks of my discovery. Radiation and chemo were not successful. She maintained her devotion to God and kept such a positive attitude. She kept many thoughts to herself, unwilling to burden her family with them. Upon learning that death was inevitable, Nan commented, "Apparently God needs me worse (than I'm needed here)." "How long do I have?" "Two weeks," was the physician's reply. "I was hoping for two months," she said.

Nan personally and individually informed her two sons of her impending death and tenderly imparted her last wishes to each of her loved ones. She counseled her youngest son not to be mad at God for taking her early (by human terms). In the midst of her beloved flower garden she sat and planned her funeral—a celebration—complete with her favorite Christmas music—in February!

In the spirit of Paul (2 Timothy 4:7-8) she fought a good fight, she finished the race, she remained faithful, and she did so with more grace and dignity and purpose than anyone could have imagined. But Nan didn't want to die. She loved life and lived it to its fullest. She wanted to experience her grandchildren growing up. She wanted to experience the wedding of her younger son. She was about to retire as head of the lab for a major hospital. She had places to go and people to see.

Believer's Bible Commentary says, "Death casts a frightening shadow over us because we are entirely helpless in its presence." We can fight pain and suffering and disease, but our strength and courage cannot overcome death. It has the final word.

It has now been six months since Nan's funeral. I am **still** researching and writing and trying to come to grips with the issue we don't want to discuss. I am recalling one of my dad's sermons that is enabling me to look at the 23rd Psalm through the eyes of its author, David. David didn't just make up words that sounded good out of his experience as a sheep herder. He **loved** his sheep. I can imagine that if one of the little guys wandered off, on the brink of trouble, David would gently scoop him up, drape him across his shoulders, and pat and comfort the little fellow as he carried him back to where he belonged. David saw to it that they were fed, watered, and protected. He

When You Find Yourself in the Belly of a Whale

totally provided for his sheep, they totally depended on their shepherd. I can envision that when one of the flock was near the end of his life, David was oh, so compassionate to the sheep he loved. He probably talked to him, tenderly stroked his little head, sang to him, played his flute for him, and never left his side—until he was no longer.

I am a believer. I recall the exact time and place that I, through faith, placed my life in God's hands. Therefore, I have a shepherd, I am his sheep. No real harm can come to me because my shepherd is in control. He will not leave my side. Even though I walk through the darkest valley, he will be there to pick me up and gently carry me into the hereafter. What more could I ask? Granted, I would rather come to the valley on my timetable. But the important thing is that when I get to that valley, my shepherd will see me through it and take me to the other side.

William MacDonald explained that unconfessed, unforgiven sin is the sting of death. But Jesus, our shepherd, took us away from that. "Now, the **worst** thing that death can do to us is really the **best** thing that can happen to us! It is true that Christians have apprehension about the suffering that often accompanies death, and it is also true that **God does not usually give us dying grace until we need it.**"

When it was obvious that death was knocking on her door, Nan's husband told her that it was okay for her to go. She didn't fight it, but closed her eyes, went into a coma, and was carried by the Great Shepherd to the place that he had prepared for her, a place with no pain, no sickness, no sorrow, forever and ever and ever.

- ❖ "The Lord is my shepherd, I have everything I need. He lets me rest in green meadows, he leads me beside peaceful streams. He renews my strength. He guides me along right paths, bringing honor to his name. Even when I walk through the dark valley of death, I will not be afraid, for you are close beside me. Your rod and your staff protect and comfort me. Surely goodness and unfailing love will pursue me all the days of my life, and I will live in the house of the Lord forever." –Psalm 23
- ❖ "I am the good shepherd. The good shepherd sacrifices his life for the sheep." –John 10:11
- ❖ "I'm asking GOD for one thing, only one thing: To live with him in his house my whole life long. I'll contemplate his beauty; I'll study at his feet. That's the only quiet, secure place in a noisy world, the perfect getaway, far from the buzz of traffic. God holds me head and shoulders above all who try to pull me down. I'm headed for his place to offer anthems that will raise the roof! Already I'm singing God-songs; I'm making music to GOD." –Psalm 27:4-6 (*The Message*)

Dr. Calvin Cantrell, pastor and retired from the Louisiana Baptist Convention, Department of Evangelism.

Believer's Bible Commentary, William MacDonald, Thomas Nelson Publishers, Nashville, TN, 1995.

THE HIDDEN BABY

The hospital had called our law enforcement agency and advised that a female had come in for medical attention. She had obviously delivered a baby but the whereabouts of the newborn were unknown. The mother slipped out of the emergency room unnoticed. We had a name. We had an address.

The temperature was freezing outside but was sweltering inside the residence. She was in bed. She knew why we were there. She offered no excuse. She offered no resistance. In response to the question, "Where is the baby? she said, "In there," and pointed to a walk-in closet. Opening the door and finding no obvious sign of life, we asked, "Where?" "In the shoe box," was her response. And there in the large boot box on the top of the chest of drawers was the baby.

I knew why we went there. And I knew what we might find. But I don't think I can put into words how it felt to hold a shoe box with what appeared to have been a perfectly healthy human life. There are a lot of "whys" surrounding the case to which we will never know the answers.

I felt compelled to write about this. Even as I write, I am asking God, "What does this have to do with anything spiritual? Why am I writing this?" And then it hit me. In the parable in which the three servants were loaned money (Matthew 25:14-30), the master only got upset with one servant, the one who hid his talents. (Talents, in today's terms, refers to our natural gifts and abilities.) "You wicked and lazy servant!" Now, does he sound highly perturbed to you? God has given us resources, talents, abilities, and time. We will ultimately answer to the Father as to what we have done with them.

Want to get personal about it? We all take issue with **time**. We never have enough of it. I once heard Dr. Shad Helmstetter explain it this way. Most Americans watch at least two hours of television per day. Multiply two hours a day by 365 days in one year. That equates to 730 hours. Now divide the 730 hours by the 40 hours of a typical work week, which adds up to just over eighteen extra 40 hour weeks a year, or just over four months. And if you watch three hours of television a day, that equates to six months.

Do you get it? When you read the opening paragraph, no doubt you passed judgment—probably even condemned the mother of the infant. Granted, there is no excuse, in my book, for what she did. Nevertheless, a sin…is a sin…is a sin. They are all the same size. They carry the same weight in God's eyes. Had we been able to prove that the baby had taken a breath of life, she would have faced a murder charge. And even if she had been found guilty here on earth, and if she subsequently confessed her sin to God and asked him to come into her life and be her Lord and Savior, she could be our next door neighbor in heaven. But what about us—our time, our abilities, our talents? When left undone, and when we answer to the Master, they carry the same penalty as a murder charge. Wow! That's tough to swallow.

God has reminded me of that on more than one occasion when I have found myself at home on the couch on extended sick leave. I am almost certain that God has used my health, or lack thereof, to get my attention regarding the misuse of his time.

So how do we set priorities? "Then Saul said, 'Let's chase the Philistines all night and destroy every last one of them.' His men replied, 'We'll do whatever you think is best.' But the priest said, 'Let's ask God first'" (1 Samuel 14:36).

Shad Helmstetter, Ph. D., personal communication, September 1997.

PLEASE, FATHER, JUST ONE SET OF FOOTPRINTS TODAY

The lumpectomy had taken place about a week earlier. It was almost time for me to meet with the surgeon for the follow-up visit. I sat in my car in the parking lot of the Doctor's Building—praying—because I feared the worst case scenario. I distinctly remember my conversation, "Father, this is one of those days when there needs to be just one set of footprints. The mental anguish of waiting has worn me down. I need to be held and carried and comforted." I took a deep breath and slowly walked inside.

My husband and one of my best friends were with me when the surgeon broke the news. "Because of the type, location, and stage of the cancer, a mastectomy will be necessary, followed by six months of chemotherapy." The thought had **never** crossed my mind, though the necessity of a little follow-up radiation had. I was numb and in disbelief. A jillion thoughts ran through my mind, though none stayed long enough for me to get a grip on them—my teaching job, sick leave, money, chemo, had he really said chemo? Of all the kinds of sickness, I hate with a passion being sick to my stomach! And I had just been sentenced to six months of it and all of those other equally fun things that go along with it.

With my background in police work, I was used to handling other people's tragedies but all three of us walked away in a daze. On one hand, I would have liked nothing better than to have crawled into a hole and cried myself to sleep. On the other hand, I didn't want to be left alone. Karen drove and I cried. I shared my fears—I even remember asking, "How am I supposed to feel?" As both a nurse and a devout Christian, Karen was able to feed me vital information and dispel some of my concerns—chemo medications are much better than they used to be, there are a number of nausea prevention medications that work. We picked up Elizabeth, the third pea in our pod, and spent the entire afternoon crying, laughing, and educating. They even helped me break the news to my parents.

Who doesn't enjoy a Friday afternoon off from work? But Paula, another dear friend, gave up a number of hers just to take me to and from chemo, and to "hurry up and wait" with me all afternoon.

Though life is full of surprises, I am so thankful that good friends remain constant. They are with you in the best of times, the in-between times, and they are with you through the worst of times. Jesus told us to love each other the same way that he loves us. He said here is the proof, "the greatest love is shown when people lay down their lives for their friends" (John 15:13). When I was in police work, backing up a partner—being willing to lay down my life for a friend had an entirely different connotation. Today, I wouldn't even trust the majority of my female friends with a gun! So, how do you lay down your life for a friend? When someone puts their life on hold for a time—their personal wants and errands, their families, their jobs—they are laying down their life for a friend.

Do you know what is even more amazing? Jesus said, in Mark 4:14-16, "You are my friends if you obey me. I no longer call you servants, because a master doesn't confide in his servants...you didn't choose me. I chose you."

Though the famous poem, *Footprints In the Sand*, isn't based on scripture, it is certainly representative of the actions of our friend, Jesus.

- ✧ "And so it happened just as the Scriptures say: Abraham believed God, so God declared him to be righteous (behaving justly; doing right). He was even called 'the friend of God.' So you see, we are made right with God by what we do, not by faith alone." -James 3:23-24
- ✧ "Rahab, the prostitute, is another example of this. She was made right with God by her actions when she hid those messengers and sent them safely away by a different road. Just as the body is dead without a spirit, so also faith is dead without good deeds." – James 3:25-26
- ✧ For the record, I don't believe that good deeds get us into heaven. But I do believe that if we are truly right with God, we can't help but do good.

FOOTPRINTS

"One night I dreamed I was walking along the beach with my Lord. Across the dark sky flashed scenes from my life. In each scene, I noticed footprints in the sand. Sometimes there were two sets of prints, other times, there was only one. This bothered me so I inquired, 'Lord, you told me you would never leave me. Why, during the lowest points in my life, are there only one set of footprints?' He replied, 'My precious child, I love you! During your times of trials and suffering—when you saw only one set of prints—that is when I carried you.' " (Author Unknown)

IT'S A TWO-WAY STREET

I was sitting in my rocking chair in my bedroom—having my quiet time with God when the whine of my Saint Bernard caught my attention. Her forehead was pressed against the window from her vantage point in the flower bed. She wanted my attention. I reached out and put my hand on the window, yet I couldn't **touch** her.

When I worked for the Sheriff's Department, now and then Metro Narcotics would need a female officer to accompany them on a drug raid. I distinctly remember one in which I was to be the third person through the door. Once inside, I was to go immediately to the television in the living room and retrieve the pistol that our informant had seen on top of it just hours earlier. How important was it to **listen** to my instructions and really understand them?

I use these unrelated scenarios to make a point. What God reveals to us through prayer and Bible study is far more important than what I say. To receive the Master's **touch**, I have to **listen**—wait for him to convey his thoughts to me. It is a two-way street.

What happens if we just stay on one-way streets in our cities? We can't always get to where we need to be. Trouble sometimes lurks there. I was on a one-way street in my police car when a lady came around the curve, going the wrong way, and struck my vehicle. A number of times, I have come to a halt at stop signs and double checked by looking the way from which cars should not be coming, and lo and behold, people were driving their cars the wrong way! (It was fairly common in our downtown area. We were located across the street from a large hospital that was visited by a number of out-of-towners, unfamiliar with our street design.)

I joke with my criminal justice students by telling them they didn't put their books under their pillows soon enough. The idea is that the information will be absorbed by the brain resulting in a good test score. (Of course, it doesn't work!)

Have you had your Bible under your pillow lately? Have you received any jolts from going down one-way streets the wrong way? Has the Master touched you recently, or is the window still closed? Did you hear what he was trying to whisper to you? Satan is always ready to raid our lives. I, for one, plan to make time daily to listen to the Master's instructions.

Oh, how human it is for us to seek advice from friends and family, when all the time, the Master is waiting for us to hear what he has to say. He uses people to support and confirm his direction, but we must be sure not to leave him out of the equation.

We expect God to get our attention with big things. Sometimes, we can only get answers when we listen for his still small voice.

- "...Listen to me, for I have excellent things to tell you." –Proverbs 8-1-12
- "My child listen to me...Then...you will know how to find the right course of action every time." –Proverbs 2:1-9
- "...Listen closely...obey...Then all will go well with you." –Deuteronomy 6:3
- "Listen to me. I created you and have cared for you since before you were born." –Isaiah 46:3
- "Each morning I bring my request to you and wait expectantly" (through prayer). –Psalm 5:3
- "And, after the earthquake, there was a fire, but the Lord was not in the fire. And after the fire, there was the sound of a gentle whisper." -1 Kings 19:12

KEEP ON WRITING! KEEP ON CALLING!

And by all means, keep on praying!

When a terrible event occurs in one's life, initially the calls and cards and other expressions of concern (books, tapes, flowers, food) are numerous. However, the visual aspects of the care and concern often fade away. Yet the pain and emotional trauma lasts for months, even years. I would strongly suggest that encouragers call or send a card at least bi-weekly. If you aren't sure what to say, select a card that says something as simple as "Thinking of You." Our church mails "We Care" cards written during the Wednesday night prayer service or in Bible Study. That is a tremendous ministry that many churches have. I never realized the value of such until I became the one in need. Little things do mean a lot. Knowing that someone took time to reach out to me and my family is invaluable. You can pick up the tangible evidence of care and concern and read it again and again to receive continued encouragement!

Being the one in need does not exempt us from being encouragers! When we reach out to others, we are meeting needs as well as momentarily removing our thoughts from ourselves.

When I was in graduate school, I took a course entitled *Death and Dying*. (Now, don't get upset. Though I've got my ticket, I'm not yet ready to ride that heavenly train, either.) I learned that any type of horrific (yes, it's a word; I looked it up!) situation can cause emotional reactions of varying degrees for two

When You Find Yourself in the Belly of a Whale

---

to five years. That includes the death of a loved one, divorce, etc. Dr. Ann Kubler-Ross stated that, after traumatic events, one can go through some or all of five stages: DENIAL, ANGER, BARGAINING, DEPRESSION, and/or ACCEPTANCE. We don't necessarily go through each stage in order. We can lapse back to a stage, though we usually don't stay in it as long on the subsequent occasions.

For close associates of a murder victim or a particularly shocking loss of a loved one, it is not uncommon for them to be unable to visualize the face of the deceased. Talk about being in the belly of a whale! If nobody shares that fact with them, they are often afraid to tell anyone out of fear that they are losing it—literally experiencing emotional problems. I have found that to be true in a few cases that I have been associated with. So there is proof that on-going, long term **I Care about you** therapy is in order.

When there are more days at the end of the month than there is money, when friends or family turn against us, when it seems like "you and me against the world" for whatever reason, we desperately need for someone to come along side of us, to cheer us on, and to inspire us to have the strength and commitment to move on.

<<<<<<<<<<>>>>>>>>>>

✧ "Give all your worries and cares to God, for he cares about what happens to you." -1 Peter 5:7

- ✧ "When you bow down before the Lord and admit your dependence on him, he will lift you up and give you honor (worth and dignity despite our human shortcomings)." –James 4:10
- ✧ "And I am sure that God, who began the good work within you, will continue his work until it is finally finished." –Philippians 1:6

Ann Kubler-Ross, M.D., *On Death and Dying*, 1969.

THE DIVERSION TACTIC

Did you ever play a sport—one you dearly loved? You'd pretty much drop whatever you were doing when someone called you to play.

You step up to the batter's box or to the golf tee. You've got on the right clothes, shoes, hat, the right bat or club. You check your swing—swoosh! In your mind you just made the hit of the year!

My husband will bound out of bed as soon as the clock goes off at 4:00...A.M.... mind you, to go sit on a piece of wood up in a tree so he can watch over the animals. (Reckon' Adam ever did that with his zoo?) He has absolutely no problem getting up to go hunting, fishing, or to play golf, but, it is awfully hard for him to part with the bed when it is a regular work day—not to mention the snooze button on Sunday mornings. The diversion from the ordinary is an amazing thing!

Think back to the woman at the well (John 4). Jesus asked her to go and get her husband. She countered with a diversion tactic. "I don't have a husband." When Jesus started revealing what he knew about her five previous husbands and current live-in boyfriend she changed the subject. She started talking about why the Jews insisted that Jerusalem was the only place of worship but the Samaritans were dead set that worship must occur at a different place. Jesus redirected the conversation. "You Samaritans know so little about the one you worship" (verse 22).

Oooooh! I could have been the woman at the well—the words applied equally to me. We've sung so many times, "The reason I live is to worship you!" But this time I was hearing it from a different point of view—the reality hit me like a ball out of nowhere. I thought, "What a mockery my life has been." Though I was driving at the time the thought struck me, mentally I was brought to my knees before my Father. If my sole purpose, the reason I live on this earth is to worship him, to praise him, to serve him, to think first and foremost of him—how wrong I have been. I am often more excited about landing on the green than I am about sharing my time with someone God has put in my path. I am often more eager to tell the tale of the "one that got away" than I am the one who died on the cross. There is absolutely nothing wrong with enjoying life—as long as the trophy is not a diversion tactic.

- ✧ "And so the Lord says, 'These people say they are mine. They honor me with their lips, but their hearts are far away. And their worship of me amounts to nothing more than human laws learned by rote.'" –Isaiah 29:13

THE SLIDE SHOW

There are times when I am teaching various aspects of Criminal Justice, particularly about child abuse and homicide cases, that for a fleeting moment, it is as if I have my own personal slide show going on inside of my head. No, it's not one you would pay money to see. The faces are filled with anger, resentment, confusion, and disbelief. The bodies are broken, bruised, and sometimes bloody. These are the cases that I worked—of real, breathing, feeling people—both perpetrators and victims.

I wonder what the Father sees. The cross, no doubt. But I think that more often the focus is on his children. I think his slide show is filled with our humanness—the fear, frustration, anger, pain, anxiety, suffering, and the mental anguish that we try so desperately to handle on our own when, all the while, he is ready to relieve us of our misery. Somehow we get it in our heads that God only needs to deal with the big stuff—we can handle the rest.

Most of us would never consider becoming a robber. Yet when we know what God expects of us and we fail to do it, we are robbing him of the opportunity, not only to bless us, but to reach out to others through us. Our stubbornness, defined as unyielding or refusing to move on, is both a hindrance to ourselves and to those we come in contact with. Is there a point of no return? There could be.

For Pharaoh there was. He led the chariot race to recapture the Israelites. Talk about a big deal! He took six hundred plus chariots and all of his horses. Each chariot carried two people—one to fight, the other to drive. (Chariots were comparable to the military tanks of today.) God parted the Red Sea and allowed the Israelites to walk to safety. But the next morning, he zapped ("looked down on from a pillar of fire and cloud, and he threw them into confusion") the chariots, causing their wheels to fall off. Can't you just see it?! —Up to twelve hundred loose wheels— and people and horses tripping over each other and then—God delivered the death penalty on Pharaoh and his entire army in the form of the current of the Red Sea (Exodus 14). (Now, that's a unique twist on capital punishment.)

The Father stands at the door of our hearts and gently knocks. He will not cause the door to open. There is only one door knob and it is on our side. Once we have invited him into our lives, he wants to help us deal with the big stuff as well as the small stuff. He wants us to pour out our hearts to him. Go ahead. He's God. He can handle it. Besides, he reads minds. We might as well be up front with him. We have nothing to lose and everything to gain. Let's get moving!

✧ "Then the Lord said to Moses, 'Why are you crying out (praying) to me? Tell the people to get moving!' " –Exodus 14:15

Life Application Bible, Tyndale House Publisher, Inc., Wheaton, Il 60819, 1991.

MANNA

We live in the country—"smack dab" in the middle of the woods, surrounded by a number of dogwood trees. Thunder had rumbled most of the night. Fairly heavy rain pounded against the house. I got out of bed, opened the vertical blinds, and to my surprise, there was what appeared to be manna all over the ground. I went to the kitchen and checked the fridge to make sure that the content of our Sunday dinner (that's the noon meal here in the South) had not changed. I thought maybe God had provided an alternate meal. The manna, originally dogwood blooms, had been knocked to the ground by the pelting rain.

Exodus 16 tells us that manna was provided to the Israelites new every morning as they wandered through the wilderness while enroute to Mount Sinai. When the Israelites first saw it, they asked, "What is it?" Moses explained that it was the food the Lord had provided for them. Eventually, it became known to them as **manna.** It was small, round, white, and tasted like wafers made with honey. It could be baked or boiled. Think about it. Forty years is a long time to eat the same thing every day (though in many countries rice is the daily staple). I suppose God could have changed the taste of it—garlic bread one day, banana nut bread the next. Or he could have given it an Italian flair one day, a Mexican taste the next, and then a Cajun twist, however—the Bible clearly says that it tasted like wafers made with honey. The people whined that they had no meat to go with the bread, so God accommodated them by sending quail for their evening meal. That happened twice—the second time was when they were leaving Mount Sinai. God had had enough of their complaining. He promised them meat—lots of it. He promised it would be enough to last a month. In fact, there would be so much that they would gag and become sick of it. God caused the wind to bring in quail from the sea. They covered the ground for miles in every direction. They flew about three feet off of the ground which enabled the people to catch them. That's a lot of birds! (The *International Standard Bible Encyclopedia* documents that quail, exhausted by migration, have been known to land on a ship in large enough quantities to sink it.) While they were still eating the meat, God became angry and caused a severe plague to break out among the people. Why? Because they kept complaining about going back to Egypt and how much better things were in Egypt and how there was meat to eat in Egypt. Did they really want to be back in Egypt? No, they just wanted an easier life. They didn't want to focus on their inability to trust God for every provision. They repeatedly failed to trust God. As a result, many died from the plague.

Other than dogwood petals, I haven't seen anything in my lifetime that comes close to manna. So of what relevance is manna and quail to our modern day? The Bible says that manna had to be gathered early every morning before the sun came out and melted it. **God always provides as the need arises. We need to begin each morning with him,**

gathering manna, before we are faced with the stresses of the day. Manna was a gift from God. It provided for the physical need of the Israelites. **Jesus is our daily bread that satisfies our spiritual need.** One could only gather enough manna for the day. Gross things happened when the Israelites disobeyed and tried to save some until the next day. Check it out for yourself in Exodus 16:20. The children of Israel could gather manna from Monday through Saturday, in modern terms. They were to double the amount they gathered on Saturday because there would be none to gather on Sunday. That was God's day off. Many of us zoom through our week, non-stop. God intended—No! He **commanded** that we rest (chill out) on the seventh day. Very few of the U.S. citizens, as a whole, are in need of food. Yes, there are some. I have actually worked cases in which I went and got food and took it back to the family. Each of us, however, is in need of a daily supply of spiritual manna. It would be so convenient if God would leave the devotional thought that we needed for the day lying around for us to find. You know, he actually does that if we just come to him each morning with our Bibles, open hearts and minds, and in a spirit of worship and prayer.

- ✧ "Draw close to God, and God will draw close to you." –James 4:8
- ✧ "From there you will search again for the Lord your God. And if you search for him

with all your heart and soul, you will find him." -Deuteronomy 4:29

✦ "Look! Here I stand at the door and knock. If you hear me calling and open the door, I will come in, and we will share a meal as friends." –Revelation 3:20

TREES WALKING AROUND

Once upon a time, in the village of Bethsaida, some people brought a blind man to Jesus and begged him to restore the man's sight. Taking the hand of the blind man, Jesus led him outside the village. After spitting on the blind man's eyes, Jesus laid his hand on him and asked, "Can you see anything now?" The man replied, "I see people, but I can't see them very clearly. They look like trees walking around." Jesus put his hands over the man's eyes a second time. This time, the previously blind man could see everything clearly. Jesus sent him on home, "saying, 'Don't go back into the village' " (Mark 8:22-27 NIV).

Strange set of scriptures, wouldn't you say? Did you wonder why the blind man wasn't called by name? Why do you suppose Jesus led him outside the village? Why didn't he just show everybody his stuff—his miraculous power? Why didn't Jesus heal the man completely the first time? Why did he use saliva to heal the guy? I'm glad you asked.

Sometimes, God has to change our circumstances in order to change us. We have to make a complete new start. You see, the man was known as "the blind man," by the villagers. He was known by his weakness. Jesus told him, in essence, don't go back in there where they'll identify you as being blind.

Initially, Jesus performed a partial healing. "**Can you see**?" Jesus asked. His reply can be interpreted to mean **sort of**. Jesus chose to do this miracle in stages, possibly, to show his disciples that some healing

When You Find Yourself in the Belly of a Whale

would be gradual. He could have been demonstrating that spiritual truths are not always understood clearly at first. Change is often gradual. Many times we are guilty of only allowing God to do just enough to give us relief but not enough to be fully delivered or totally healed.

What if—our hearts are changed? What if—our sight changed? The church has been given the duty of reconciliation—forgiving, letting go, making peace. The church is given the task of seeing the world through the Father's eyes—as living, breathing, human beings. Unless scripture has changed—the church—that would be me and you!

- "Then Jesus said to him, 'Don't tell anyone about this. Instead, go to the priest and let him examine you. Take along the offering required in the law of Moses for those who have been healed of leprosy. This will be a public testimony that you have been cleansed.'" -Matthew 8:4

Beth Moore, *Woman to Woman* Conference, Memphis, TN, June 2001, adapted from conference notes.

THE DUTIES INCUMBENT UPON ME

Had I known what those words would encompass, I'm not sure that I would have said, "I do." An officer is sworn to uphold the laws of the state in which s/he resides as well as the laws of the United States—but donning a swimsuit, getting on an air mattress, and paddling across the bayou to buy drugs from some dude on the pier???? My comment to the narcotics agent proposing this undercover tactic was "water and wires don't go together." Then it occurred to me that swimsuits leave no room for concealed weapons either. He assured me that they would be watching with binoculars and if the deal turned bad—I guess they'd come running across the top of the water to rescue me.

Whatever! (I learned I was pregnant about that time so the deal never came to be. Whew!)

Keeping in mind that incumbent means binding, obligatory, a duty—what are the duties incumbent upon me as a Christian? Some duties are generic to all of us. Others are specific to each of us as individuals.

Peter was a great example. Re-create his life's story with me. (Warning: My version differs somewhat from actual scripture.) I love Simon Peter because he was so human—so much like us. He grew up fishing on the Sea of Galilee so it was natural that he and his brother, Andrew, would take on fishing as a trade. He was not highly educated. He lived in a town called Bethsaida. He was married (Mark

1:30) and, after Jesus called him to the ministry, his wife was known to travel with him (1 Corinthians 9:5). Looking in the Cylopedic Index of my Bible, this is what I find about Peter. He was brought to Jesus by his brother, Andrew, at which point, Jesus changed his name to Cephas (meaning Peter or rock). (How would you like it if somebody you had just met decided to change your name?) Peter was then called to discipleship (thus the reason for the name change). Jesus saw him for what he would become—the duties that would be incumbent upon him. Peter walked on the water—failed at that and got all wet. He and the other disciples realized that Jesus was the Messiah (Matthew 16:13-19). And lo and behold, two verses later, he gets in trouble. They now knew that Jesus' cause could never fail—that no matter what they were on the winning side. Then Jesus decided to break the news that he had to go to Jerusalem and that he would be killed but he would be raised to life three days later. This made Peter indignant at the thought of his Master enduring such treatment. Check this out. He pulls a defense tactic move—on Jesus (Matthew 16:22). He caught hold of Jesus as if to block his path. "Never Lord, this shall never happen to you," Peter said. And Jesus fussed at Peter for his line of thinking. You see, when Jesus was tempted by Satan in the desert, he was told that he could be great without dying (Matthew 4:6). Here, Peter is implying the same thing—he knew he was the Messiah but he was looking at the situation through human eyes. "Get behind me, Satan! (Jesus said to Peter.) You are a stumbling block to me; you do not have in mind the things of God, but the things of men" (Matthew 16:24). Satan is always trying to get us to leave God out of the picture. In calling Peter "Satan," Jesus did not mean that he was demon-possessed or controlled by Satan. He just meant that Peter's actions and words were what could be expected of Satan. Peter just needed a little attitude adjustment. His deep love and devotion to Jesus blinded him from the truth.

We need to be cautious when friends attempt to assure us that God doesn't want us to suffer or face certain situations. Sometime those are the duties incumbent upon us—the very things(s) that will take us to a deeper dimension with him. —The thing that will enable us to minister to others going through similar situations. I wouldn't have chosen cancer as a way to minister anymore than Jesus would have chosen the cross—had there been another way.

If you find yourself angry at the world, bitter at the system, cynical—if you just don't enjoy your "job," question your call. If you are just doing a job, ask God if he wants to change it to your calling. If not, he may have another profession waiting in the wings for you. Or you could be experiencing the down time as apart of spiritual time-out—the time when God is pruning you so that you may bloom where he has planted you.

I do know that Peter didn't have it all together even after his attitude adjustment. Back to the Biblical Index: He cut off a man's ear in an effort to protect Jesus, then he denied even knowing Jesus, not once, but three times; he wept bitterly; he healed people, he preached his heart out—-to the point of going to jail over and over for it. He went from rookie status as a disciple to enlightened and humble, from timid and afraid to fearless. He became a leader. He penned two books to comfort us, to challenge us to live holy lives, to show us how to keep the faith in the midst of our sufferings, to give us courage as we go about life—performing all of the duties that are incumbent upon us.

- ✧ "Peter and the other apostles replied: 'We must obey God rather than men! The God of our fathers raised Jesus from the dead, whom you had killed by hanging him on a tree. God exalted him to his own right hand as Prince and Savior that he might give repentance and forgiveness of sins to Israel. We are witnesses of these things, and so is the Holy Spirit, whom God has given to those who obey him. When they (the Sanhedrin, 70 men/council/court) heard this, they were furious and wanted to put them to death. But a Pharisee, named Gamaliel, a teacher of the law, who was honored by all the people, stood up in the Sanhedrin and ordered that the men be put outside for a little while...I advise you to leave these men alone! Let them go! For if their purpose or activity is of human origin, it will fail. But if it is from God, you will not be able to stop these men; you will find yourselves fighting against God. The others accepted his advice. They called in the apostles and had them flogged. Then they ordered them never again to speak in the name of Jesus, and they let them go. The apostles left the high council rejoicing that God had counted them worthy to suffer disgrace for the name of Jesus. And every day, in the Temple and from house to house, they continued to teach and preach this message: 'Jesus is the Messiah.' " –Acts 5:29-42

✧ "What blessings await you when people hate you and exclude you and mock you and curse you as evil because you follow the Son of Man." –Luke 6:22

Believer's Bible Commentary, William MacDonald, Thomas Nelson Publishers, Nashville, TN, 1995.

I'M NOT BELIEVING MY EARS!

Just suppose you were roaming around the back forty (as in acres of land) when, out of nowhere, you could declare that you heard the trusty old horse under your saddle SPEAK. I'm talking words, not just some equine sound. And what's worse, you find yourself answering the beast! What's a guy to do? Pick up his cell phone and call the local shrink? Promise himself not to tell a single soul? Or maybe just abandon ship (so to speak) and while walking back to the barn calculate the animal's potential value at the sale barn.

Well, would you believe it happened for real one day? Yep! Sure did, somewhere between 1450-1410B.C. How do we know? Moses wrote it down in Numbers 22. Do you remember the children of Israel? The ones that wandered around for forty years. At this point, the old generation has died and the younger generation is camped out in the plains of Moab, east of the Jordan River, across from Jericho. They are finally ready to inhabit the Promised Land. It seems as though Balak, the king of Moab, was quite disturbed. "Look. A people has come up out of Egypt, and they're all over the place! And they're pressing hard on me." He sent a message by his emissaries to a sorcerer named Balaam along "with the fee for the cursing tucked safely in their wallets. Come and curse them for me—-they are too much for me. Maybe then I can beat them; we'll attack and drive them out of the country" (Numbers 22: 2-14).

When You Find Yourself in the Belly of a Whale

I suppose you could say that Balaam walked on both sides of the fence. He was both a sorcerer and a prophet. Though he had some knowledge of the true God, he frequently engaged in heathen practices, calling on gods and magic to invoke curses on people. In essence, God told Balaam, "Don't go there. Don't curse those people because I have blessed those people." Did he listen? Well, no!

"Balaam got up in the morning, saddled his donkey (okay, it wasn't a horse) and went with the princes of Moab. But God was very angry when he went, and the angel of the Lord stood in the road to oppose him. Balaam was riding on his donkey, and his two servants were with him. When the donkey saw the angel of the Lord standing in the road with a drawn sword in his hand, she turned off the road into a field. Balaam beat her to get her back on the road. Then the angel of the Lord stood in a narrow path between two vineyards, with walls on both sides. When the donkey saw the angel…she pressed close to the wall, crushing Balaam's foot against it. He beat her again. Then the angel of the Lord moved on ahead and stood in a narrow place where there was no room to turn, either to the right or to the left. When the donkey saw the angel of the Lord, she lay down under Balaam, and he was angry and beat her with his staff. Then the Lord opened the donkey's mouth and she said to Balaam, 'What have I done to you to make you beat me these three times?' Balaam answered the donkey, 'You have made a fool of me! If I had a sword in my hand, I would kill you right now.' The donkey said to Balaam, 'Am I not your own donkey, which you have always ridden, to this day? Have I been in the habit of doing this to you?' 'No,' he said. Then the Lord opened Balaam's eyes and he saw the angel of the Lord standing in the road with his sword drawn. So he bowed low and fell face down. The angel of the Lord asked him, 'Why have you beaten your donkey these three times? I have come here to oppose you because your path is a reckless one before me. The donkey saw me and turned away, I would certainly have killed you by now, but I would have spared her' " (Numbers 22:21-34).

Do you know what the moral of this story is? Actually, there are several. God can be as creative as he needs to be to get a point across. Not only don't you have to be a perfect person, you don't even have to be a person for God to use you. The donkey saved Balaam's life but made him look rather foolish in the process, so Balaam lashed out at the donkey. Don't we sometimes lash out at blameless people when we are embarrassed or our pride has been hurt?

Just for the record, I have a few other questions about ol' Balaam. Why would God use a sorcerer? God has a message for the Moabites. They had already decided to hire Balaam. So God used him, just like he used the bad pharaoh to accomplish his will in Egypt. Did Balaam remain a good guy? No, he didn't. Later scriptures show that he liked the money and idolatry too much to give up.

Eugene Peterson, *The Message*, 2002.

Donna Partow, *Becoming a Vessel God Can Use*, Bethany Press, Bloomington, MN 55438, 2004.

Life Application Bible, Tyndale House Publisher, Inc., Wheaton, Il 60819, 1991.

BATTLE READY?

How quickly the Miranda Rights can fly from the mouths of us law enforcement professionals. How expeditiously we can read the riot act to the citizen who has gone astray. And how easily we can quote portions of the Criminal Code (the law book), complete with the title and sub-section (exactly where it can be located). We become so familiar with it that we commit it to memory. We learn to interpret it and how to apply it to a variety of situation.

If you were a law enforcement officer, I would ask, "Can you **quote** more **law** or more **scripture**?" If you were a music lover, I would ask, "Do you know more **lyrics** from **memory**, or more **scripture**?" If you were an avid watcher of movies or television, I would ask, "Can you **quote** more lines from **movies** or commercials, or more **scripture**?"

Beth Moore wrote, "Scripture is the only weapon we have against the evil one. The other pieces of armor described in Ephesians 6 are **defensive** in nature."

When Jesus was taken into the desert and was tempted by Satan, he finally (after forty days) won that battle by quoting scripture. And Satan "didn't tuck his tail and run the first time Jesus drew the Sword of the Spirit (scripture)." Why should we think Satan would treat us any differently?

As we do life—simply go through our routine activities—we are tempted, tested, and tried. How do we prepare for battle in this arena? Just as firearms training at the police academy prepares us for the gun battle we hope we never find ourselves in, so does studying and memorizing scripture prepare us for sword fighting with the enemy—none other than Satan, himself. A Bible Concordance is a great tool for locating Bible verses related to particular situations. Books await you in Christian bookstores that have re-worded verses of scripture into prayers.

As a sidebar, could we back up and note one interesting fact? Luke 4 says, "Then Jesus, full of the Holy spirit, left the Jordan River. **He was led by the Spirit to go out into the wilderness, where the Devil tempted him…**" Did you catch that? Who led him to be tempted? The Holy Spirit! Sometimes we feel that if the Holy Spirit leads us to do anything that it will be "beside quiet still waters" (Psalm 23:2). But that is not necessarily the fact. He may lead us into trials and difficult situations. When we find ourselves in this position, we need to, first, search ourselves to see if there is any sin to confess or any behavior that we need to change. If that is not the issue, then we must be careful to ask our heavenly Father to give us the strength we need to fight the battle. Remember, Satan often chooses to fight immediately after low points in our lives. Why? Because we are much more vulnerable at that point.

DEATH BY GUNSHOT

In the aftermath of the Littleton, Colorado, shooting, Michael W. Smith recorded a song in honor and memory of Rachel Scott. It was Rachel who stood up for her belief in god, and it cost her life.

This was the song.
This was the dance.
Live every moment.
Leave nothing to chance.

This was truly an example of a modern day persecution. We would all like to think that, if faced with the same choice, we would respond in the same manner.

As criminal justice professionals, we go to the firing range and train extensively for a day when we may find ourselves looking down the barrel of a gun. At my department, we had to sign for a time slot, well in advance. I am firmly convinced that the training/range officers should post the Farmer's Almanac or extended weather forecast along with the sign-up sheet. You know the routine: "Be here come rain, hail, sleet, shine, or snow." I had the opportunity to qualify in the snow and sleet once—in Louisiana! I had numerous opportunities to shoot the targets with the rain dripping off of my nose and gun barrel. And then one day, my partner and I knocked on a door—in the rain. The suspect hollered out, "I'm not coming out alive." My first thought—"**who dies?**"

My second thought—"**Well, at least we know we can shoot in the rain!**"

When I came face to face with death by way of cancer, I found myself pondering—No!—wrestling with the issue of death. I have been a Christian for over thirty years. I've got my ticket, I'm just not ready to ride. I have life yet to live, things not yet accomplished. I don't relish the thought of a painful death. But most of all, I'm not ready to leave my family and friends.

As Christians, we sing about heaven, talk about entering through the pearly gates, joking with Saint Peter, and walking on the streets of gold. It almost seems a contradiction that, in the face of death, I, a Christian, of all people, don't want to go. Psalm 23 days, "Even when I walk through the dark valley of death...your rod and staff...comfort me." Yet all of my inner being was crying out "but I'm not comforted!" Is it okay to feel that way? Is something wrong with my Christianity? What would Jesus think. I wrote in another devotional, I don't think he minds me questioning, but I do think he wants me to investigate it enough to come to grips with it.

I don't know about you, but when I am struggling to work through an issue, it seems that God makes his message known in several ways through a number of sources. The day after I was reminded of Rachel's commitment by hearing the song on the radio, I was on my way to work when it hit me. **What is the difference?** The manner in which Rachel died was a tremendous testimony of her faith. God used her death to get his message to a lot of people. He used her family to model forgiveness to the rest of the world. What is the difference if I die by gunshot or by cancer, if that is the way God chooses for me to bring hope to a dying world?

Even though I walk through the darkest valley of death, he will be there to pick me up and gently carry me until I am strong enough to stand again or carry me through to the other side. Granted, I would rather have a choice in the matter as to when my work on earth is finished, but my Father knows best. In fact I would like it if, when my time comes, I just got taken up into heaven, like Elijah and Enoch (2 Kings 2:11 and Genesis 5:23-24). When you fly the Jesus way, there is no pain.

The bottom line is, we are all terminal, you know!

- ✧ "Jesus told him, 'I am the way, the truth, and the life. No one can come to the Father except through me.'" –John 14:6
- ✧ "Our earthly bodies, which will die and decay, will be different when they are resurrected, for they will never die." – 1 Corinthians 15:42

WHAT'S THE PRICE ON YOUR HEAD?

In other words, how much are you worth?

I was chaperoning a trip in Canada when my husband received the call. The secretary for our Criminal Investigation Division had received an anonymous telephone call which revealed that a **hit** had been placed on my life, pursuant to one of my homicide investigations. The amount of money that would be exchanged for my life was never disclosed, but I'm **sure** it would have been thousands—even millions!

In an unrelated case, I had been sued for 1.6 million dollars. (Of course, they didn't get it!)

What is the price on your head?

Dave Dravecky, former pitcher for the San Francisco Giants, lost his pitching arm and shoulder to cancer at the pinnacle of his career. He stood before our congregation. With his baseball card in the one hand he had, he folded the card in half, creased it with his lips, and used his teeth to hold the card while he tore it in half. There, on the card, was half of a man. How valuable was Dave's card when he no longer had a pitching arm or stats? How valuable was he to his family when his means of support was suddenly taken from him?

Do we have value and worth apart from our jobs and the committees and organizations we represent? Criminal justice professionals are a strange breed. We tend to eat, drink, sleep, and breathe the criminal justice system—the excitement of it, the boredom of it, the fears and aggravations of it. Book him today; he's back out tomorrow. We tend to hang primarily with others in the criminal justice system. Why? Because they experience and understand the same frustrations that we do. This is known as the police subculture. It gives rise to high rates of alcoholism, suicide, and divorce.

If you were a criminal justice professional, I would ask, what is your value apart from how many arrests you make or cases you clear, or how many probationers/parolees you successfully rehabilitate (or not)? To others, I would ask you to associate it to your work-related duties.

What is your worth as a spouse? As a dad or mom? A friend? A child of God? I guess I am asking, where are your priorities? God's plan says God should be first. Hold a place for your family, second, and others should be third.

- ✧ "And he will give you all you need from day to day **if you** live for him and **make the kingdom of God your primary concern**." –Matthew 6:33
- ✧ "Then Saul said, 'Let's chase the Philistines all night and destroy every last one of them.' His men replied, 'We'll do whatever you think is best.' But the priest said, '**Let's ask God first.**'" -1 Samuel 14:36
- ✧ "Not even a sparrow, worth less than a penny, can fall to the ground without your Father

knowing it...you are more valuable to him than a whole flock of sparrows." –Matthew 10:29

✧ "For God loved the world so much that he gave his one and only Son, so that everyone who believes in him will not perish but have eternal life." –John 3:16

✧ "And what do you benefit if you gain the whole world but lose your own soul?[a] Is anything worth more than your soul?" –Matthew 16:26

NETWORKING

Yeah! Yeah! You know what it is. When women do it, it is **gossip**. When men do it, it is called **networking**. It's all of those hearsay tidbits of information that we leave with and promptly share with others.

So what's the point? Words, our speech, can be powerful tools of destruction. Yes, they can build us up, but that's not my point. I'm talking about the trouble we cause ourselves and others because of it.

Consider this: The average horse weighs in the vicinity of a thousand pounds. Certain breeds boast of weighing up to a ton. James, the brother of Jesus, wrote, "we can make a large horse turn around and go wherever we want by means of a small bit in its mouth" (James 3:3). James wrote to Jewish Christians who had been scattered throughout the Mediterranean world because of persecution. They were treated like the bad guys. Some, like Stephen, were even stoned to death. Meeting together in a church could get one killed. So James wrote letters to encourage them in their faith.

Apparently, the issue of speech was a big deal. It warranted 12 versus of James' letter (recorded in James 3, almost at the end of the Bible). Maybe he was concerned that his readers wouldn't get the significance of the "tongue" issue that he was addressing, so he painted them another word picture. "And a tiny rudder makes a huge ship turn wherever the pilot wants it to go, even though the winds are strong" (verse 4). The Queen Elizabeth weighed 83,673 gross tons. The rudder of the ship weighed in at only 140 tons—less than two-tenths of one percent of the total. "So also, the tongue is a small thing, but what enormous damage it can do" (verse 5). James continued, "It only takes a spark, remember, to set off a forest fire. A careless or wrongly placed word out of your mouth can do that. By our speech, we can ruin the world, turn harmony to chaos. Throw mud on a reputation, send the whole world up in smoke and go up with it, smoke right from the pit of hell." Whoa! Did you get that? Satan, the devil himself, uses the tongue to divide people, to pit them against each other. Once untrue or hateful words are spoken, the damage has been done.

Do you remember hearing about the historical event involving Mrs. O'Leary's cow? They lived in Chicago. It was in the year 1871. It seems as though the cow kicked over a lantern and started a fire that burned for three days over three and a half square miles of the city. Two hundred fifty people died, 100,000 were left without a home, and property valued at $175 million was destroyed. Whether or not that tidbit of information is true, we do not know. But, we do know, the tongue has the potential to do just as much damage.

James says the tongue can defile the whole body. Clovis Chappel wrote, "...The mudslinger cannot engage in his favorite pastime without getting some of the mud that he slings both upon his hands and upon his heart...Yet, that was not our intention at all. We were vainly hoping that by slinging mud upon others we might enhance someone's estimate of our own cleanliness. We were foolish enough to think we could build ourselves up by tearing another down... we always inflict deeper injury upon ourselves."

And finally, James says, "People can tame all kinds of animals and birds and reptiles and fish, but no one can tame the tongue" (verse 7). James probably penned these words around A.D. 49. I'm not sure that they had circuses and Sea World's and rodeos back then, but given sufficient time and persistence, probably every species of wild animal could be trained. Yet, man cannot tame the tongue.

The Message, a contemporary rendering of the Bible from the original language puts it this way. "This is scary. You can tame a tiger, but you can't tame a tongue—it's never been done. The tongue runs wild, a wanton killer. With our tongues we bless God our Father, with the same tongues we curse the very men and women he made in his image. Curses and blessings out of the same mouth! My friends, this can't go on. A spring doesn't gush fresh water one day and brackish the next, does it? Apple trees don't bear strawberries, do they? Raspberry bushes don't bear apples, do they? You're not going to dip into a polluted mud hole and get a cup of clear, cool water are you?" (James 3:7-12).

Well, I guess that brings us to the question: If no human being can control the tongue, why bother trying? We can't, but God can. 'Fess up. He knows we've got a problem but he wants to hear us admit it. He'll convict us within our own minds and enable us to hold our tongues. Can I anticipate having a totally clean mouth from now on? Unfortunately, not while on this sinful earth. But we can make a huge difference in the lives of other by praying daily that the Lord will keep us from gossip, networking, and unkind speech.

Believer's Bible Commentary, William MacDonald, Thomas Nelson Publishers, Nashville, TN, 1995.

COMPLEMENTARY OR CONTRADICTORY?

On the first day of my judicial process class, I throw out for discussion the words **Criminal Justice**. Do the words go together? Do they complement each other? Or are they directly opposed? I have a good idea of what you are thinking. I've been in the system, as we say, for quite some time (since 1976, to be exact).

Most of us have skeletons, of some sort, in our closets, meaning we've done, said, or failed to do things that we are not very proud of. We would prefer to push them to the recesses of our minds, close the door, and leave them there. Satan, on the other hand, likes nothing more than to sneak them out of the closet and right back before the very eyes of our soul. I hate it when he does that—making me feel guilty all over again for something for which God has already forgiven me.

1 John 1:9 says, "But if we confess our sins to him, he is faithful and just to forgive us and to cleanse us from every wrong." Yet, Satan keeps impressing upon me that in order for justice to be truly served, I deserve to pay for—to suffer for—my sins. Don't I deserve to pay for my sins just like criminals pay for their crimes? After all, I am guilty.

Romans 3:23 and following read, "But in our time something new has been added. What Moses and the prophets witnessed to all those years has happened. The God-setting-things-right that we read about has become Jesus-setting-things-right for us.

And not only for us, but for everyone who believes in him. For there is no difference between us and them in this. Since we've compiled this long and sorry record as sinners (both us and them) and proved that we are utterly incapable of living the glorious lives God (wants) for us, God did it for us. Out of sheer generosity he put us in right standing with himself. A pure gift. He got us out of the mess we're in and restored us to where he always wanted us to be. And he did it by means of Jesus Christ. God sacrificed Jesus…to clear the world of sin. Having faith in him sets us in the clear" (*The Message*).

Another version of the Bible says, "For all have sinned and come short of God's glorious standard. Yet now God in his gracious kindness declares us not guilty. He had done this through Christ Jesus, who has freed us by taking away our sins. For God sent Jesus to take the punishment for our sins and to satisfy God's anger against us. **We are made right with God when we believe that Jesus shed his blood, sacrificing his life for us.** Can we boast, then, that we have done anything to be accepted by God? No, because our acquittal is not based on our good deeds. It is based on our faith. So we are made right with God through faith and not by obeying the law…"

The law was not given to justify (save, salvage) people. Thank goodness, because nobody is able to keep it. Its purpose was to serve as a standard—so we would know that we don't measure up. **We could never be good enough to get into God's heaven.**

Think of it this way: We could never know what a crooked line is unless we also knew what a straight line looked like. If we are to walk the straight and narrow, the law serves as the straight line by which we measure ourselves to see how crooked we are. William MacDonald, in his commentary wrote, "We can use a mirror to see that our face is dirty, but the mirror is not designed to wash the dirty face." By the same token, a thermometer will confirm that one has fever, but it will do nothing to reduce the fever. The law produces "conviction of sin, but it is worthless as a savior from sin." As Luther said, its (the law's) function is not to justify but to terrify."

We (Christians), unlike criminals, don't have to pay our debt to society for the wrongs we have done. Look at the word **just**. Its origin, *dikaios*, means "that one conforms in his actions to his constitutionally just character. The rules are self imposed." You see, justice is a standard that is too high for us. **We could never behave in a manner that totally fulfills God's expectations of us** (Romans 3:10). **Had it not been for Jesus on the cross of Calvary, forgiveness and justice could never co-exist. That would be a contradiction of terms. "We would be hopeless; our confession of sin could bring only a 'just' verdict: guilty—and a swift sentence: death." Though he did not sin, Jesus took on himself all of my sins and all of your sins.**

Imagine yourself standing before the celestial (heavenly) court, scared to death, knowing you should be sentenced to hell—but Jesus takes the witness stand—he takes the rap on your behalf.

When You Find Yourself in the Belly of a Whale

You, my friend, have been acquitted—**just for the asking**! ☺

✧ "So where does that put us? Do we Jews get a better break than the others? Not really. Basically, all of us, whether insiders or outsiders, start out in identical conditions, which is to say that we all start out as sinners. Scripture leaves no doubt about it:

> There's nobody living right, not even one,
>   nobody who knows the score, nobody alert
>   for God.
> They've all taken the wrong turn;
>   they've all wandered down blind alleys.
> No one's living right;
>   I can't find a single one.
> Their throats are gaping graves,
>   their tongues slick as mudslides.
> Every word they speak is tinged with poison.
>   They open their mouths and pollute the air.
> They race for the honor of sinner-of-the-year,
>   litter the land with heartbreak and ruin,
> Don't know the first thing about living with
>   others.
> They never give God the time of day.

This makes it clear, doesn't it, that whatever is written in these Scriptures is not what God says about others, but to us to whom these Scriptures were addressed in the first place! And it's clear enough, isn't it, that we're sinners, every one of us, in the same sinking boat with everybody else? Our involvement with God's revelation doesn't put us right with God. What it does is force us to face our complicity (accomplice; partnership) in everyone else's sin." –Romans 3:9-20 (*The Message*)

✧ "This is how much God loved the world: He gave his Son, his one and only Son. And this is why: so that no one need be destroyed; by believing in him, anyone can have a whole and lasting life. God didn't go to all the trouble of sending his Son merely to point an accusing finger, telling the world how bad it was. He came to help, to put the world right again. Anyone who trusts in him is acquitted; anyone who refuses to trust him has long since been under the death sentence without knowing it. And why? Because of that person's failure to believe in the one-of-a-kind Son of God when introduced to him." –John 3:16-18 (*The Message*)

PUT OUT TO PASTURE

I had heard the term "put out to pasture" all of my life, but I'm not sure I really understood until fairly recently. You see, Zack came to live with us as a favor to a friend. We discovered that Zack has an attitude problem. In fact, he is just down right ornery. The old boy has the tendency to kick. He doesn't have to be provoked, he just does it. He practically demolished his own stall in that he kicked numerous windows of opportunity (when he had the opportunity he made a hole) in its sides. So Zack went out to pasture. In other words, he is permanently banned from the barn. Doesn't seem to bother him. I've observed him kick the fire out of the pasture fence and the fence didn't do a thing to provoke him! It was just standing there.

And then, there is ***Tait's Royal Angel***. She's a 3 year old. Beautiful! Intelligent! Easily trained. Other than her female, adolescent attitude, she's fine. She, too, got put out to pasture, at least temporarily. Why? She bites ***Peppy***—just because. *Peppy's* tail is quite a bit shorter, thanks to Angel. She doesn't bite Zack. But the main reason she has been put out to pasture is there is plenty for her to eat.

Buster and I walk in the evenings (as in exercise). Day after day, as we pass by the back pasture, Angel comes running, or at least she speaks. She wants our attention. She enjoys the back pasture, but she misses the companionship.

Isn't that the way it is with us and God? Sometimes we put ourselves out to pasture. It is quiet and away from the hustle and bustle, yet, after a while, we find that something is missing. As Blaise Paschal put it, "we have a God-shaped vacuum within." Our heavenly Father, through the Holy Spirit, put it there to cause us to miss him—

to cause us to want to spend time with him—to draw us to him or back to him.

We can never run far enough that God loses sight of us. We can never get so far that he cannot hear us. And we could never get so far back in the pastures of our lives that he forgets we are there. Want proof? In Psalm 139:1-12, David told God of his discovery, "...even in darkness I cannot hide from you." Romans 8:38 tells us that "nothing could ever separate us from his love." Notice that the scripture doesn't say "well, nothing except...could separate us." The way I figure it, nothing means absolutely nothing!

Have you noticed that the way something is worded makes all of the difference in the world? Being **put** out to pasture seems to have somewhat of a negative connotation. But if I said "**let** out to pasture," how would that hit you? Ah, now that is a privilege. Let me share what the prophet Malachi said (Malachi is one of those books that is in the back pasture—if you're looking for it, go to Psalms and turn right; it's the last book in the Old Testament.)

The Lord God Almighty says, "The day of judgment is coming, burning like a furnace. The arrogant and the wicked will be burned up like straw on that day. They will be consumed like a tree...roots and all. But for you who fear (revere, respect) my name, the Son of Righteousness (prophecy later fulfilled by Jesus Christ) will rise with healing in his wings. **And you will go free leaping with joy like calves let out to pasture.** On the day when I act, you will tread upon the wicked as if they were dust under your feet"

(Malachi 4:2-3).

Now that's what I'm talking about! The book of Malachi forms a bridge between the Old and New Testaments. It promises hope. When we trust God with our lives, we can look forward to a joyful celebration.

NOW, THAT'S A SCARY THOUGHT

Mind reading! We joke about it. There are games that make you think it can be done. Spouses and friends become so close that, on occasion, they can tell what the other is thinking.

My mind runs 90 m.p.h. with gusts of up to 120 m.p.h. My students tell me that my rate of speaking is not far behind. Though my thoughts run in a variety of directions, God knows what I am thinking. He even knows the motive behind the thought. Ooooooh! That could be *not* a good thing.

I've read Luke 7:36-50 a number of times, but the mind reading thing had never really occurred to me until recently. The Scripture tells of a Pharisee named Simon that invited Jesus over for dinner. They had barely gotten in the door when an immoral woman just invited herself right in. In those days they didn't have street people shooting up drugs in the alley, so she was likely a prostitute. It was a custom of the time for people to recline while eating. Dinner guests would lie on a type of couch. They would prop up on their elbow with their heads near the table while they stretched their feet out behind them. The intruder brought with her a beautifully carved jar filled with expensive perfume. She was discrete, meaning she was quiet and wasn't up in Jesus' face, since his feet were stretched out behind him. As tears began to trickle down her cheeks—and on to Jesus' feet, she gently wiped them away with her long flowing hair. The source of her tears was not the fact that she was an immoral woman, a prostitute—rather, they flowed out of a deep sense of love for Jesus because she had been **forgiven**. She continued to rub the feet of her beloved Jesus with the fine perfume.

When the master of the house saw what was happening, he didn't say a word. No! But he thought to himself, "Well this proves it. Jesus is no prophet because had God really sent him he would know the background of the immoral woman that is touching him. He'd put a stop to this." No sooner had the thought gone through the Pharisee's mind than Jesus "**spoke up and answered his thoughts**" (verse 40). Whoa-ho!

Granted, there are numerous points that could be gleaned from this scripture. The mind reading is the one that catches my attention, though it's not the one we usually focus on. Psalm 139 says, "O Lord, you have examined my heart and know everything about me. You know when I sit down or stand up. You know my every thought..." Sometimes I am glad that he knows my heart—even my good intentions that never came to pass. Other times, I am utterly embarrassed.

Beth Moore, in her prayer journal, *Whispers of Hope*, suggests that each morning we ask God "...for an immediate awareness when (we) are departing His authority," It stands to reason that if God knows what I'm thinking, then it's o.k. for me to bring up my thoughts, both good and bad, to him. That honesty—that transparency—is the only way to build an intimate relationship with him. Why shouldn't I tell him if I am angry or feel that life is being unfair or if

I'm scared, hurt, or whatever? After I face up to the feeling by verbalizing it to him, only then can he help me deal with—understand, work through—the issue. And yes, sometimes the situation remains the same, but my attitude toward it changes.

✧ "Summing it all up, friends, I'd say you'll do best by filling your minds and meditating on thing true, noble, reputable, authentic, compelling, gracious...the best, not the worst; the beautiful, not the ugly; things to praise, not things to curse...Do that, and God, who makes everything work together, will work you into his most excellent harmonies."
–Philippians 4:8-9 (*The Message*)

Beth Moore, *Whispers of Hope,* LifeWay Press, Nashville, TN, 1998.

HOOK, LINE, AND SINKER

Think about it in light of the awesome power of God. Throughout Elisha's ministry, God used him to do some incredible things. He parted the Jordan River so he could get to the other side (2 Kings 2:7). Wouldn't it have been easier for God to allow Elisha to walk across the top of the Jordan? God used him to purify water for drinking and crop production. He allowed Elisha to increase a widow's oil (2 Kings 4:2-7). God enabled Elisha to bring another widow's son back to life (2 Kings 4:18-36), to neutralize poisonous soup so that it would not kill those who ate it (2 Kings 4:38-43), to multiply bread, heal one leper (2 Kings 5): 1-19) and inflict leprosy on another (2 Kings 5:20-27). He caused an iron axe head that had fallen into the Jordan River to float so that it could be found (2 Kings 6:1-7). God used him to open the eyes of some to see the mighty army that God had provided to fight and he struck the Aramean army with blindness (2 Kings 6:8-23). Get this, even after Elisha was dead and in the tomb, he was still causing miracles. "Once while some Israelites were burying a man, suddenly they saw a band of Moabite raiders, so they threw (the body of one of the raiders) into Elisha's tomb. When the body touched Elisha's bones, the man came to life and stood up on his feet" (2 Kings 13:21). Wow! What a God!

Elijah and Elisha are the two most notable prophets (proclaimers of God's message) of the thirty mentioned in the Bible. Elijah was a fiery character that confronted and exposed idolatry and was instrumental in creating an atmosphere where people could freely and publicly worship God. You may remember him as the one who had the fiery showdown with priests of Baal (1 Kings 18:25-40). When Elijah was taken to heaven in a whirlwind, Elisha picked up where he left off and performed many miracles to put the people in touch with the powerful, yet caring and compassionate, God.

My friend, the truth is that God is the same yesterday, today, and tomorrow. He is still in the miracle business. Miracles are performed in our world on a regular basis, for those who have the faith and ability to see them for what they are. He can work them in our lives and he can use us and the things that happen to us to lay foundations in the lives of others so that much can be accomplished for him. He is the power source. We are the tool. Remember, **we are on this earth to further his kingdom, not our desires**. When we allow God to assume his rightful place as God in our lives, he can do some phenomenal things in and through us.

How does one plug into the awesome power of God? Kay Arthur said in *Speak to My Heart, God*, "The devil is having a heyday among Christians today because through one means or another, he's blinding them to who they are in Christ. Satan is feeding them a lie, and they're swallowing the bait—-hook, line, and sinker..." Just for the asking, God will **forgive you of your sins** and come into your life, making you a brand new creature. You **don't have to fear death**, because you are not going to die until God wants you to. And then, you will immediately be present with your heavenly Father. As his child, you are encouraged to "**come boldly to his throne**" to tell God what you need. God promised to "**supply all of our needs**." He's done all he can do. Now it is up to you.

- *Forgive you of your sins*:

    o *God loves you*: John 3:16
    o *You are a sinner:* Romans 3:23
    o *You are dead in sin:* Romans 6:23
    o *Jesus Christ died that you might live:* Romans 5:6-8
    o *You can be saved by faith:* Acts 16:30-31, Ephesians 2:8-9
    o *You can know you are saved from hell:* 1 John 5:10-13
    o *You are now his child and are to obey him:* Acts 5:29

- *New creature*: Romans 6:4-7, 2 Corinthians 5:17, Galatians 2:20
- *In heaven with God*: 2 Corinthians 5:8-9, Revelation 1:18
- *Boldly to his throne*: Hebrews 4:16
- *Supply all of our needs:* Matthew 6:33, 1 Corinthians 3:21-23, Philippians 4:19

To find scripture, log on to: www.Biblegateway.com

Kay Arthur, *Speak to My Heart, God,* Harvest House Publishers, Eugene, Oregon 97402, 1993, p275-6.

THE SOUND OF SILENCE

I would venture to say that for most that is not a welcome sound—silence.

Many are comforted by the background noise of music or the television. Some admit they don't like being quiet. I love it. I can stay at home all day without either—just my thoughts running around in my head. Yes, there are times when my own thoughts get on my nerves and I have to ask God to rescue me from them.

Now, I'm sitting here in the early morning trying to put on paper (o.k. the computer!) what God is inspiring me to write. My husband just got up and greeted me and immediately I heard him talking to someone on his speaker phone while preparing breakfast—microwave beeping, cabinet and refrigerator doors opening and closing, television news informing, etc.—just the routine on-going of life. I am thinking "focus, focus." Silence can be most difficult to find and achieve even when we are searching for it.

Think about the relationship of God and man. The psalmist questioned God, "O LORD, what are human beings that you should notice them, mere mortals that you should think about them? For they are like a breath of air; their days are like a passing shadow." *The Message* says it this way: "I wonder why you care, GOD— why do you bother with us at all? All we are is a puff of air; we're like shadows in a campfire" (Psalm 144:3-4).

Well, I'll tell you why. God loves you intimately—more than anyone on earth could ever love. He created you and he put a lot of thought and effort and detail into you. Psalm 139:13-18 reveals his love for you: "You made all the delicate, inner parts of my body and knit me together in my mother's womb. Thank you for making me so wonderfully complex! (Think about the complexity of your brain and how your bodily organs function together.) Your workmanship is marvelous—how well I know it. You watched me as I was being formed in utter seclusion, as I was woven together in the dark of the womb. You saw me before I was born. Every day of my life was recorded in your book. Every moment was laid out before a single day had passed. How precious are your thoughts about me, O God. They cannot be numbered! I can't even count them; they outnumber the grains of sand! And when I wake up, you are still with me!" (He is so fond of us he wants to be with us all of the time!)

Jeremiah 29: 11-13 says, "For I know the plans I have for you," says the LORD. "They are plans for good and not for disaster, to give you a future and a hope. In those days when you pray, I will listen. If you look for me wholeheartedly, you will find me."

The Message poignantly expresses the same scripture this way: "Yes, when you get serious about finding me and want it more than anything else, I'll make sure you won't be disappointed."

He knows us by name. He keeps up with the number of hairs on our heads—that just means he cares about the smallest details of our lives. Stands to reason that he would be equally concerned about the little things that burden us as well as those we consider insurmountable.

Why, then, do we fear silence? Could it be that when we really get quiet we have to deal with ourselves? That is when God can begin to reveal things that need to be changed or rearranged. Hammond said, "Intimacy automatically breeds revelation, and revelation will always demand change in our lives." So we get busy to avoid having to deal with this—stuff. **AND THEN WE WONDER...where is God** when I need him?!

Why can't I hear him?

Hammond explained it so beautifully: "When we spend time with God and learn to really be still and listen, we hear him saying, I am Peace. I am Provision. Ultimately, I am God. I've got it. I've got your back. I've got this situation it the palm of my hand."

Remember the saying, "I don't know what tomorrow holds, but I know who holds tomorrow."

Michelle McKinney Hammond, *Fear of Silence*, excerpted from the *Be Still* DVD.

IT'S IN BLACK-AND-WHITE

Renee and I had gone to work at 8:00 in the morning. During the course of the day it became necessary to obtain a search warrant on a case we were working. Finally, at 3:00a.m.—the next morning—we were on our way home. We lived in close proximity to each other so the plan was for me to drop Renee off at her residence. We were tired, anxious to get home, and were moderately exceeding the speed limit. As we rounded the last curve—we both saw them. Lot's of them. Black and white spots everywhere. Who knew that our local dairy farmer paraded his cows across the road at 3:00 in the morning? But there they were in **black and white**. Needless to say, we hit the brakes rather hard and sat there bug-eyed with mouths hanging open until we got a mental grasp on what was happening before our very eyes!

Would you believe that black-and-white is in the dictionary? It means completely, either one way or another, without any intermediate state—unlike the cows!

One cannot help but notice what a corrupt society we live in. Corruption is rampant within police departments, politics, business deals, and the list goes on and on. To some it is an expected and accepted way of life. That's not the way God sees it! To him the way of life is black-and-white.

I just received my new Code of Criminal Procedure, from which I teach various aspects of law. If something is against the law in the State of

Louisiana, it is in that book. I can't help but wonder what happened. God gave Moses the law on two tablets of stone—ten little laws—actually commandments (Exodus 31:18). I just measured our current book of laws to be just over 1 ¾" thick. What's the deal? Our society deemed it necessary to put in black-and-white the legal procedures and specific elements of each crime, as well as the penalty for each. We have all sorts of variations for most laws.

I am currently undergoing testing to determine if I have cancer of the pancreas.

A serum marker test is negative for cancer. My physician, however, explained that is not conclusive. The cyst could still be cancerous or contain pre-cancerous matter. Continued testing is necessary. In fact, we may have to "watch it for a couple of years." It is not black-and-white. At times I begin to think, what if the next test is positive?

We wrestle with all sorts of **what if** issues. What if I lose my job? What if this relationship continues to go downhill? What if my child continues to hang with the wrong crowd? What if my parents suffer from Altzheimers? God is probably thinking what part of do not worry do you not understand? You see, he wrote it in black-and-white. "Don't worry about anything; instead, pray about everything. Tell God what you need, and thank him for all he has done. Then you will experience God's peace, which exceeds anything we can understand. His peace will guard your hearts and minds as you live in Christ Jesus (Philippians 4:6-7).

THIS IS NOT THE LIFE I SIGNED UP FOR

I really did not want to include this chapter of my life in this book. It is too painful! But God says I must, therefore, I must!

After undergoing a mastectomy and chemo (1999-2000), I tended to think "goodness—that's enough stuff to last a lifetime. So glad all of this has happened to me at such a young and tender age. Now I can sit back and enjoy life." The kids were in college so we had an empty nest.

You no doubt recall September 11th—the terrorist attack on the U.S. All of us were devastated and in shock that such could happen to us right here on our own turf. Two days later my husband of 27 years made a surprise announcement that he was leaving. The next day he moved out and to another town. He had gone on a mission trip a few months before and left to pursue a relationship with one of the women that had been on the trip.

The divorce was much worse emotionally than the cancer. Though I've never been through it, I personally think it would be much easier for a spouse to die than to desert. Desertion devastates and cuts to the very core of one's being. You question, blame yourself, become angry. When it seems you can't go on—you must attempt to pick up the shattered pieces of what is left of your life.

It wasn't just my crisis. The kids were a big mess. Family and friends were shocked. My husband was a deacon, interim music director, Bible teacher, choir president—everything he stood for he had turned from and that was especially confusing and heart breaking for the kids.

Three weeks after my he left, my mom and dad decided that if I was going to live alone in the country, I needed a German Shepherd. I brought the cute, furry seven week old little creature into the house and introduced her to my three year old 13 pound cat named Simon P. (I've mentioned him elsewhere in *When You Find Yourself In The Belly of a Whale*. Do you remember how the biblical character Simon Peter was characterized as sometimes being in a little trouble? He sank while walking on the water, he cut off the ear of Malchus in an effort to keep Jesus from being arrested, then he denied Jesus three times, etc.) I left the puppy and cat in the floor checking each other out while I turned to put my purse on the bar. The puppy seemed to be thinking, "Great, I have a new friend." And the cat just stood in awe at the creature that was invading his space. I thought, "Good! This isn't going to be so bad," when I began to hear a low pitched growl coming from Simon P. Realizing that he was not a happy camper, I picked up the puppy and turned my back on Simon P. thinking "OK, one critter over there and one critter over here will give them time to get used to each other." Wrong! Without further notice, Simon P. came up my back and over my head. I began to hear pounding on my head and feel a burning sensation on my face and then to see significant amounts of blood making great spatters upon the floor when I finally came to realize I was under attack! I bent forward, still cradling the puppy with one hand, and grabbed a handful of Simon P. with the other hand, threw him to the floor and rushed out the back door. (The puppy was the intended target. I just got in the way.) I looked like I had been thrown the windshield of a car, but thirteen stitches, 8 staples, and numerous steri-strips later I'm all healed up with only hints of scars.

At that point, I was really feeling a lot like Jobette (a female version of Job!) My daughter called. "Mom, go get your "Streams in the Desert" devotional book and turn to page seven." And there, I discovered my new life's verse. Job 42:12 says, "So the Lord blessed Job in the 2nd half of his life even more than in the beginning." Yes! You can claim that verse, too, if you need to.

And if that were not enough, about three months later one cold, cold day, I had a roaring fire in the fireplace. My mom was assisting me in bringing in firewood at dusk. I had a mumbo jumbo load stacked in my arms when I tripped and fell forward leaving both thumbs lodged in the wood which were trapped beneath the weight of my body! Are you aware of the limitations of having no useful thumbs? Try pulling pants up and down, buttoning blouses, and turning door knobs for starters.

I was sitting at a red light a few months later when someone rear ended me. (No big deal, thank goodness!)

Having been blind-sided by a massive storm of life—Hurricane Katrina size, and then another—Hurricane Rita size—and yet another, I began to wonder "where is God in all of this? Has he moved and left no forwarding address for me? What is the deal?

I've said before, I wondered if I was blessed or cursed. I wondered if God gave Satan permission to sift me? I wondered if I was such a threat to Satan that he felt it necessary to attempt to get me to blame God thus creating disharmony.

When things like these happen, we are not out of line doctrinally to assume that the same huge competition that Job encountered, takes place all around us. You and I have no idea what's going on in the unseen world when we're being attacked. But, we do know who wins in the end. The author of *When Godly People Do Ungodly Things* says when the heat is on she tells herself, "This could really be important. Stand firm and don't give the (cheer) leaders of hell anything to cheer about. God is **for you**."

Donna Partow, author of *This Isn't The Life I Signed Up For* asks, "Isn't it hard to fathom that God is always for us? If he is, then why does he let our opponents hit us so hard?" Among other reasons, could it be to prove that we, mere mortal flesh and blood, terribly self-centered by nature—really are for God. **That no matter how hard or how many times the enemy strikes, I will not relinquish my praise of and dependence on my God!**

Some of us may say, well, I've already blown it. I flunked the test. Let me ask you. Who among us hasn't. Jesus once said, "Let he who is without sin cast the first stone," knowing full well that we've all blown it. That's why he did what he did on the cross. Paul wrote, "No, dear brothers and sisters, I have not achieved it, but I focus on this one thing: Forgetting the past and looking forward to what lies ahead, I press on to reach the end of the race and receive the heavenly prize for which God, through Christ Jesus, is calling us (Philippians 3:13-14). Or as it says in The Message, "I'm off and running, and I'm not turning back" (verse 14b).

This isn't the life I signed up for! I had the plans for my future in a nice, neat little stack in my head, and this chain of events isn't in them. Clearly, this is not the life I signed up for. I would do well to remind myself that God is quite capable of picking my little train up and putting it back on track. " 'For I know the plans I have for you,' says the LORD. 'They are plans for good and not for disaster, to give you a future and a hope' " (Jeremiah 29:11).

Beth Moore, *When Godly People Do Ungodly Thing*, Lifeway, 2002.

Donna Partow, *This Isn't The Life I Signed Up For*, Bethany House Publishers, 2003.

CAT AND DOG PERSPECTIVES

When a thunderstorm is approaching, our big Saint Bernard stands whining and barking outside the back door. If I'm not mistaken, she's saying, "Can't you see what is about to happen. Pleeeze, let me in. I'm scared to death." (She does have a nice cedar Saint Bernard-size house, complete with carpet.) On the other side of the door sits Simon P., the big white cat. From his vantage point, he sees all of the leaves and pine needles sailing by in the wind, so he begs for us to let him out so that he may give chase. There are times when we open the door. Simon P. bounds out on to the deck then realizes it is cold and wet—not what he expected. He turns around and comes back in but continues to voice his displeasure. When he's in, he wants out; when he's out, he wants in. It's all a matter of perspective.

If only we could view the happenings in our lives from God's vantage point. It would be much easier getting through the crisis of the moment if we knew how God would provide, where it would lead and when we would get there. Why do you suppose God chooses to keep that privileged information? Could it be that he has some life lessons and spiritual maturity to teach us? Indeed, he does.

Where does faith fit into this conversation? There are those whose faith is based on signs, like Gideon (Judges 6: 36-40) when he put out the fleece in order to get a sign (or confirmation) from God to ensure that he was getting the message from God that he

When You Find Yourself in the Belly of a Whale

thought he was getting. (Whew! Did you get that?) While we may not put out a literal fleece today, we may look for a sign or proof in circumstances or what people say. Yes, God speaks through people and he certainly speaks through his word, the Bible.

Cowan said **the deepest level of faith, the one that transcends all other levels, enables us to believe God and his word when circumstances, people, emotions, appearances, and human reasoning all seem to urge something to the contrary.**

The 27th Chapter of Acts presents the thrilling saga of the voyage of Paul and fellow prisoners being shipped to Rome. (The true stories found in Acts rival any fiction or true story that I've ever read!) The weather was treacherous because it was the fall of the year. Many days of traveling had been slow. In fact, Paul told the officer in charge of the prisoners, to no avail, "I believe there is trouble ahead if we go on—shipwreck, loss of cargo, and danger to our lives as well" (verse 10). "When a light wind began blowing from the south, the sailors thought they could make it. So they pulled up anchor and sailed close to the shore of Crete. But the weather changed abruptly, and a wind of typhoon strength (called a "northeaster") burst across the island and blew us out to sea. The sailors couldn't turn the ship into the wind, so they gave up and let it run before the gale (verses 13-15). The terrible storm raged for many days, blotting out the sun and the stars, until at last all hope was gone" (verse 20). Without the ability to see the sun and stars, there was no way to get their bearings as to where they were and which direction they needed to head. Sailors bound the hull of the vessel with ropes to strengthen it, threw excess cargo overboard, they lowered the anchor to slow the speed, but the wind continued to batter the ship. Finally Paul called the weak, tired, hungry, scared, and hopeless crew together and gently reminded them that if they had listened to him in the first place they wouldn't be in this mess. Paul wasn't taunting them. He was letting them know that, with God's guidance, he had predicted what would happen. Needless to say, in the future, when he spoke—they listened. "But," he said, "take courage! None of you will lose your lives, even though the ship will go down. For last night an angel of the God to whom I belong and whom I serve stood beside me, and he said, 'Don't be afraid, Paul, for you will surely stand trial before Caesar! What's more, God in his goodness has granted safety to everyone sailing with you.' So take courage! For I believe God. It will be just as he said. But we will be shipwrecked on an island" (verses 22-26).

As the ship began to tear apart and sink, all who could were ordered to swim to shore. The rest were told to grab boards and float to shore. Not one of the 276 passengers aboard perished.

Check this out: Some of the natives of the island saw the shipwreck and had witnessed the victims struggling to get to shore. In a hospitable gesture they gathered wood and built a fire to warm and dry them. Apparently a poisonous snake had taken refuge in a piece of driftwood and when it was placed upon the fire the snake quickly exited and in his fear and anger struck out at the first thing he saw—poor ol' Paul! (If

When You Find Yourself in the Belly of a Whale

that doesn't sound like something that would happen to me—!) The snake latched on to his hand—not in a coil but with a bite, mind you! Paul didn't die but the ensuing story is well worth the read (Acts 28).

You see, God still had work for Paul to do in Rome. Since he had quit persecuting and killing Christians, Paul frequently became the hunted. He seemed to incite problems among the Jews everywhere he went so they found a way to keep him in jail. Subsequent to numerous court appearances, Paul appealed his case to Ceasar. God made a way when there seemed to be no way. Where was Ceasar's court? In Rome, of course.

Can you see how Paul exhibited that deepest level of faith? Nothing—absolutely nothing gave credence to Paul surviving in order to get to Rome—he was hunted, jailed, starved, shipwrecked, and bitten by a poisonous snake!

A couple of months ago I had a hiatal hernia repair and had only been back at work for three days when I began to feel terrible. I spent Thanksgiving, plus a few days, in the hospital under the threat of having to get a blood transfusion and take a kidney to prevent my losing blood. There was talk of masses and cancer and clots. Numerous prayer chains were immediately activated and that entire medical problem resolved as being nothing more than a blood clot. THANK YOU, LORD and THANK YOU PRAYER WARRIORS! My doctor doesn't understand. I gave him the answer—a lot of people were praying. He never acknowledged God's part in the resolution. I've been hospitalized a number of times, and that was not normally the hospital I have used. Was I shipwrecked over there for that physician to witness our deep faith and a miracle? I think there is a good chance. I know that I was an emotional basket case for a few days, which drove me back to re-reading and adding to this manuscript. Oh, how God uses our faith to accomplish his purposes!

Note the confidence of the worshiper in Isaiah 26:3-4, "You will keep in perfect peace those whose minds are steadfast, because they trust in you. Trust in the Lord forever, (for the Lord is everlasting strength)." No doubt, the faith of this writer had been strengthened from experiencing God's deliverance and provision. You know, a sense of peace is not determined by our circumstances, but by our state of mind. By focusing more on who is in control and whose plan is unfolding, we are given a totally different perspective from what is going on in the world around us.

L.B. Cowan, *Streams In The Desert*, Zondervan Publishing House, 1997.

OH, GOD!

Does the phrase *Oh, God* conjure up visions of George Burns and John Denver from the move by that title? Is that the cry that comes from your lips to summon his help when you realize you are in the middle of what could easily turn in to a major mess? Or is it a phrase that is flippantly used merely as an expression?

I challenge you to **listen** for a day—at the grocery store, around the office, in the lunch room—where ever you happen to be. Listen for the word **GOD**. Catch the manner in which it is used. You might even check your own conversation.

The backdrop for this writing came from overhearing a teenage girl in the hallway at our Wednesday night church activities. She **wasn't** summoning the Master. I thought, "I wish he (God) would just **poof**! —and appear right there beside her. His words could be 'you called?' " Maybe a better analogy would be Moses and the burning bush—but most of us don't recall seeing that one. At any rate, a little reality therapy might do us all good.

People are often known for the little things they desire. For example, a golfer may live for a game like Tiger Woods. An entrepreneur is usually consumed by a higher profit margin. A pistol team competitor longs for the perfect score every time. When we back off and look, the things we seek reveal the passion and priorities of our hearts. "Our chances of accomplishing our goals increase in (direct) proportion to the intensity of our commitment. Remarkably, the Bible (says) it is possible for human beings to know and experience the God of the universe in a personal way. He desires an intimate and transforming relationship with..." each of us (Touch Point Bible). In order for that to happen, we have to seek after him—pursue him—with the same focus and intensity that we would use to win a trophy or make that extra money. The Bible challenges us to ask ourselves, "Is God just one among (my) many pursuits, or is (he) chief of all (my) desires?"

Oh, how I wish I **could** whisper his name and he would visibly appear right beside me—to share my conversation and thoughts, to give me advice and guidance, to just hang out with and have fun, and wouldn't I love to go fishing with him! Somehow, that's not the mental picture we have. What **does** the scripture say about our Savior? Well, he was the kind of guy you would want to be around. That means he was fun, likely humorous—scripture teaches that a cheerful heart is like a good medicine (Proverbs 17:22). Beth Moore says, "Fishermen don't leave their nets to follow someone void of personality. People didn't just respect him—they liked him." And kids! Jesus was an advocate for them. He liked kids. In Matthew, Chapter 18, it seems that the disciples were arguing among themselves about which of them would be the greatest in heaven, of all things! Jesus used a living object lesson to make his point. He called a child over to stand beside them. "I'm telling you, once and for all, that unless you return to square one and start over like children, you're not even going to get a look at the kingdom, let alone get in...if you give them a hard time, bullying or taking advantage of their simple trust, you'll soon wish you hadn't. You'd be better off dropped in the middle of the lake with a millstone around your neck" (The Message).

Jesus wasn't tricking! To emphasize his point, He even mentioned the fact that God's children (adults that belong to his kingdom included) have angels in the presence of our heavenly Father, waiting to protect and rescue us when necessary (Matthew 18:10). Jesus took it one step further to let us know that these little guys are so special that if even 1 out of 100 of them got lost, s/he is valued and respected enough for a search party to be sent out. Yes, that's the one I'm summoning when I say, "Oh, God!" You see, to him—we (you and me) are that little kid!

✧ "Then he took the children into his arms and placed his hands on their heads and blessed them." –Mark 10:16

Beth Moore, *Jesus, The One and Only*, LifeWay Press, 2000.
Eugene Peterson, *The Message*, NavPress Publishing Group, Colorado Springs, CO, 1995.
Touch Point Bible, Tyndale House Publishers, Wheaton, IL, 1996.

THE LAND OF THE GIANTS

It was God's plan to give the Israelites the Promised Land (Canaan). About three years after escaping Egypt, they arrived. You would think that when they finally caught sight of it they would have almost run over each other in an effort to step foot on—to take possession of—the land promised to them by God, himself. But no! Though God had delivered them from Egypt, parted the Red Sea and had seen them safely through to the other side, fed them with bread from heaven, and literally guided them with a cloud—still they didn't take him at his word. What a people!

They wanted to check it out. So God told Moses to send in twelve spies (Numbers 13). Moses plotted the direction they were to take. He told the men to find out if the inhabitants of the land were weak or strong. He wanted to know if their towns were surrounded with walls or if they were unprotected. The spies were to check out the land. What type of soil did it have? Were there a lot of trees? And they were to bring back samples of the crops.

It happened to be the season for harvesting grapes. The spies cut a cluster of the luscious fruit that was so large it took two men to carry it out on a pole between them. I would say the land had promise, wouldn't you? After 40 days of exploration, the men felt they had gathered sufficient information and returned with their report.

The land is "indeed a magnificent country—a land flowing with milk and honey," they told the people, as evidenced by the huge grapes. The cities and towns are very large with great walls of protection. Among the people are giants—literally. Two of the spies were confident that they (the Israelites) would be victorious in taking the land. They saw the situation through eyes of faith. The Israelites, however, took issue and were convinced they were as "grasshoppers" that would be devoured by the inhabitants of the land. God didn't take too kindly to their unbelieving attitude. In fact, God initially vowed to wipe out that group of people and raise up a new nation from Moses' descendants. He relented and **in essence** said, "Fine! I'll let you live but you will wander in the wilderness for 40 years until the unbelieving generation has died." He vowed that of the 603,550 men 20 years of age and older who came out of Egypt, only Caleb and Joshua would eventually enter the Promised Land.

Did Giants really exist in the days of old? Yes. Scripture gives us specifics on a couple of them. King Og's iron bed was more than thirteen feet long and six feet wide according to Deuteronomy 3:11. And remember Goliath (1 Samuel 17:4). David, the shepherd boy took him out of this world with a pebble and a sling shot. He topped out at nine feet nine inches tall.

Are giants still around today? Emphatically, yes! They are the difficulties that surround us. We encounter them within our households, our workplaces, in various relationships, and even in our churches. If we fail to overcome our giants, they will either devour us, just as the Israelites feared the inhabitants of the land would do to them, or they will cause us to wander aimlessly, as did the children of Israel.

Each of us, at some time, is temporarily overloaded by life's circumstances. We usually find a way to manage. "It is when there is a convergence of life circumstances extended over time that we can begin a downward spiral of becoming emotionally disconnected," according to authors Ray and Nancy Kane. That chronic state of being overwhelmed causes us to feel as though we are dying inside emotionally. That "means that we experience the fears of failure, rejection, and abandonment at the same time and with the same intensity." We experience the paralysis of emotional overload. "We automatically become emotionally handicapped (which) means that the degree and amount of unresolved pain in our lives significantly outweighs the pain we have resolved.... We either withdraw or wait for others to take responsibility for our unwillingness to deal with our pain.

Some of us suffer chronic and debilitating diseases that claim our quality of life. *Journey* contained the testimony of one who has suffered from the **giant** of rheumatoid arthritis for 20 years. She is forced to use wrist splints and special grips to grasp the handles of pots and pans. She said she must choose daily whether to give her pain and discouragement to her heavenly Father or to sink into the pit of despair.

Great difficulties are our giants. Many think that the power of God in our lives should keep us from

When You Find Yourself in the Belly of a Whale

facing great difficulties. Not so. We encounter giants **when** we are serving and following God. *Streams In The Desert* implores us to look at the Israelites. They encountered the giants while enroute to the Promised Land but when they retreated, the giants were no longer an issue.

How can we know we have faith, until our faith is tested? "God trains his soldiers, not in tents of ease and luxury but by causing them to endure lengthy marches and difficult service. He makes them wade across streams, swim through rivers, climb mountains, and walk many tiring miles with heavy backpacks." Charles Spurgeon asks, "Could this not account for the difficulties you are now experiencing?"

Cowan explained, "Difficult times and places are our school of faith and character. If we are ever to rise above mere human strength, and experience the power of the life of Christ in our mortal bodies, it will be through the process of conflict that could very well be called the 'labor pains' of the new life."

L.B. Cowan, *Streams In The Desert*, Zondervan Publishing House, 1997, p149 and 254.

Ray and Nancy Kane, *From Fear to Love: Overcoming the Barriers to Healthy Relationships*, Moody Publishers, 2002.

Journey-A Woman's Guide to Intimacy With God, LifeWay, November 2007.

GREAT IS THY FAITHFULNESS

Each and every time I have gone through one of life's difficulties, I have been reminded of the old hymn *Great Is Thy Faithfulness*. In fact, I seemed to hear it so much in various places, I called it my theme song. Allow me to share how the first verse and chorus are interpreted in the depths of my soul.

Great is Thy faithfulness, O God my Father;
Father, every time I find myself feeling like I am in the belly of a whale, there you are. Sometimes I imagine my face buried in your shoulder, as you hold and comfort me through my tears. Other times I feel as though you are just sitting with me while I am waiting—for medical tests, healing of body or relationship or processing the challenge of the moment to the point of acceptance. At times it seems you must be guiding my hands and thoughts to various writings or scripture from which I can find comfort and grow spiritually. But Father, you have always been there with me.

There is no shadow of turning with Thee;
Some have called into question your love for them because you allowed a difficulty or loss to occur. Others believe that your power should keep any hint of conflict or trials from happening at all and they quickly wash their hands of you and throw in the towel, so to speak, wanting nothing more to do with a God who is useless to them. But Father, regardless

of what happens or how bad life seems, I'm hanging on to you for dear life. My hope is in you. I realize life on this earth is not what it is all about. I'm simply passing through on my way to an eternity with you — free of heartache, illness, frustrations.

Thou changest not, Thy compassions, they fail not;
We are so human and have all acted unwisely and hurt others, though often not on purpose. We have good intentions but many times find ourselves not making time for each other. While people and places and things on this earth are forever changing, you, Oh, Lord, are always the same — caring, compassionate, and accessible.

As Thou hast been, Thou forever will be.
I don't ever have to worry about you, God. You will always be the same.

Great is Thy faithfulness!
You are stable, dependable, devoted.

Great is Thy faithfulness!
You are reliable and trustworthy.

Morning by morning new mercies I see.
It's not only in major life events that I've encountered you. Every single day I discover new ways that you have shown kindness and compassion to me. You bless me over and over again. You have shown favor to me. You have taken me under your wing.

All I have needed Thy hand hath provided;
There is nothing I have **needed** that you haven't made a way for me to get or provided for me.

Great is Thy faithfulness, Lord, unto me!
Oh, God, your devotion to me is more than I can comprehend.

Thomas O. Chisholm penned the words of the poem *Great Is Thy Faithfulness* in 1923. He said there was no single event that led to the writing but a culmination of his experiencing the truths of the Bible. It became a hymn in that same year when William M. Runyan set the words to music.

As I think of how indebted we are to these gentlemen for giving us this great hymn of faith, I ponder our generation's legacy upon those who come behind us. Will our stories and writings and songs inspire them to seek and worship the God of our fathers, whom we know to be so very faithful? I also wonder how many of us have sung those words countless times and have never taken to heart the depth of love and compassion and faithfulness he has exhibited to us as individuals—unconditionally accepted and loved. It has been asked, "If your life were the only book others read, would they see Jesus in you?" How are you handling the crisis of the moment? Will your friends and family attest to the fact that God saw you through? Or do you need to invite him into your life and allow him to be God?

Of this one thing I am sure—**my God is faithful!**

<<<<<<<<<<◇>>>>>>>>>>

- ✧ "The faithful love of the LORD never ends! His mercies never cease.
- ✧ Great is his faithfulness; his mercies begin afresh each morning." –Lamentations 3:22-23
- ✧ "God's loyal love couldn't have run out, his merciful love couldn't have dried up.
- ✧ They're created new every morning. How great your faithfulness! I'm sticking with God (I say it over and over). He's all I've got left." –Lamentations 3:22-23 (*The Message*)

Hope Publishing Company, http://www.cyberhymnal.org/htm/g/i/gisthyf.htm, January 31, 2008.

ALL IS WELL — AT LEAST ON THE INSIDE

She was a missionary to Brazil for 17 years but returned stateside to raise five children when her husband's life was claimed by a drunk driver. That's when I met my current best friend. *It Is Well With My Soul* was one of the songs she chose to have sung at his funeral. How could it be? She had to find a place to live and a job. Not only was she dealing with the loss of her husband of 28 years, but she had grieving children who had never even lived in the United States.

Horatio G. Spafford, a wealthy businessman, experienced financial ruin after the great Chicago Fire in October 1871. Not long thereafter, Mrs. Spafford and their daughters were crossing the Atlantic Ocean on the *S. S. Ville de Havre*, when it collided with another ship. All four of the Spafford's daughters died. Soon after, Horatio, boarded a ship enroute to meet his beloved Anna. As his ship neared the location where his daughters perished, the Holy Spirit inspired the words to *It Is Well*.

When peace, like a river, attendeth my way,
When sorrows like sea billows roll;
Whatever my lot, Thou has taught me to say,
It is well, it is well, with my soul.

It is well, with my soul,
It is well, with my soul,
It is well, it is well, with my soul.

*Though Satan should buffet, though trials
   should come,
Let this blest assurance control,
That Christ has regarded my helpless estate,
And hath shed His own blood for my soul.*

Though experiencing anguish after reliving her experience through testimony, I have heard Sherry belt out *It Is Well With My Soul* with all the conviction she could muster. What's the deal? No matter what physical pain or emotional trauma we may experience on this earth, God is more than able to give a peace that passes beyond human comprehension. It rests in the knowledge and assurance that heaven is a far better place than we could ever imagine. And one day, because of accepting Jesus' free gift of salvation, we will reunite with our loved ones. Oh, what a day that will be!

- ✧ "I pray that God, the source of hope, will fill you completely with joy and peace because you trust in him. Then you will overflow with confident hope through the power of the Holy Spirit." –Romans 15:13
- ✧ "So also Christ died once for all time as a sacrifice to take away the sins of many people. He will come again, not to deal with our sins, but to bring salvation to all who are eagerly waiting for him." –Hebrews 9:28

- ✧ "Look! I stand at the door and knock. If you hear my voice and open the door, I will come in." –Revelation 3:20
- ✧ "And he died at a ripe old age, having lived a long and satisfying life. He breathed his last and joined his ancestors in death." –Genesis 25:8

Hope Publishing Company, http://www.cyberhymnal.org/htm/g/i/gisthyf.htm, January 31, 2008.

SO YOU WILL KNOW

And so I won't forget!

I was reading a devotional thought by Luci Swindoll (the sister of Chuck) in which she encouraged would be writers to just start putting something down on paper. I began to jot a few thoughts in a notebook but rarely brought any to completion.

Shortly thereafter, I walked with my husband through a fifteen month mid-life crisis. During that time, I desperately needed to let out what I was feeling. Consequently, I went back to my notebook and scribbled the emptiness and brokenness on to the pages.

I was subsequently diagnosed with cancer and impending surgery and chemotherapy. My daughter was on foreign mission field for the summer. While awaiting her early return due to my health, I was browsing through a book store in the New Orleans International Airport when *Just Enough Light for the Step I'm On* caught my eye. It is about *Trusting God in the Tough Times*. Stormie Omartian shared the struggles she encountered before finally asking God what he wanted her to do. She clearly knew that she was to write. She bought a desk and writing supplies and sat down every day and waited for the Lord to show her what to write. She is now a noted speaker and author of books, song lyrics, and numerous magazine articles.

Stormie wrote that if you feel that God is leading you in a particular direction he will confirm it though a praying believer. I remembered that to be consistent with what Henry Blackaby taught in *Experiencing God*. The day after I read Stormie's statement, an acquaintance from my church called to check on me after the surgery. I did not know her well but I did know her to be a powerful woman of prayer. Her statement was, "You know, you need to be writing down all of these thoughts." I knew that God meant business! He had given me thoughts before that I never followed up on. In my busyness, I had neglected to make it a priority. Had he put me in time out again to get my attention?

And so, devotional titles began to pop into my mind. I have learned to take a small notebook everywhere I go so that I will not lose the trains of thought God gives to me via every day life. Sometimes the thought come to me in the middle of the night. I've asked God if it could wait 'til morning, but I just got up and wrote them down without waiting for his answer! One morning he gave me forty eight devotional titles. In January 2000, I began to make time almost every day to sit down with my Bibles, and commentaries, look at the devotional titles, and begin to write on one until it was completed, sometimes over a several day period. As I wrote, it developed. How long did each devotional take? On the average, about three to four hours. I have noticed one thing that is **so God**. I am a stickler for details, largely due to my background as a Criminal Investigator. I have the "if it isn't in your report it didn't happen" mentality. I have noticed that God freely allows me to hit the delete key. I'm not obsessed with what I think should be written, but with what God puts in my head to write.

Have you heard Beth Moore speak? Every listener comes away from her conferences saying "she is anointed." She can get things that we've never thought about out of the same scriptures that we have all read over and over. Why? Because she is anointed. She is called by God; set apart for a specific purpose.

When I look back at some of the things I wrote during the mid-life crisis they are so shallow. They ramble. They are unfinished. I was not anointed. Since God obviously wants me to write, I have fervently prayed for him to cleanse me and give me the words to meet the needs of his people, just as the words of others that have touched my life. I don't pray to be like them. They are human. I pray for God to anoint me so that I can write his words, just as Paul and Luke and Moses and the others.

✧ "Such things were written in the Scriptures long ago to teach us. They give us hope and encouragement as we wait patiently for God's promises." –Romans 15:4

Stormie Omartian, *Just Enough Light for the Step I'm On-Trusting God I the Tough Times,"* Harvest House Publishers, Eugene, Oregon 97402, 1999.

CHARTREUSE

Chartreuse! That was my son's favorite color, even before he was old enough to spell it. (To be honest, *spell check* told me I didn't know how to spell it either. Who knew it had an "e" in it?) Adam was recently married. The beautiful brown bridesmaids dresses were accented with—chartreuse! It is a special shade of green—but it isn't really green. It is—well—chartreuse! The dictionary defines it as a strong to brilliant color.

I love bold, brilliant colors. (It is so like God to select the perfect bride for Adam—right down to her love of chartreuse!)

The Bible speaks of the color red. Well—not really red, but crimson. Some versions refer to it as scarlet. The dictionary defines crimson as a deep, vivid purplish-red.

Scripture says, "Come now, let us argue this out," says the Lord. "No matter how deep the stain of your sins, I can remove it. I can make you as clean a freshly fallen snow. Even if you are stained as red as crimson, I can make you as white as wool" (Isaiah 1:18).

Crimson was a deep red permanent dye. It was virtually impossible to remove from clothing. One Bible commentary tenderly explained that "we don't have to go through life permanently soiled" because of our sin, no matter how bad we think it was.

I witnessed a perfect analogy of God's grace and forgiveness. While snow skiing in Colorado, we were on a lift headed to the top of a mountain. From our vantage point we had a birds-eye view. One skier was hastily making his way down the ski run from about the 11:00 o'clock position and another was wasting no time traversing downward from about the 2:00 o'clock position. It was obvious that if each maintained his speed, their paths were destined to meet—and it was not going to be a pretty sight. Just as we feared, the inevitable happened. The blanket of white snow was greatly tarnished with a significant amount of crimson, if you know what I mean. The next morning as we headed to the top of the mountain by way of the same lift, it was impossible to tell where the collision had occurred. New fallen snow had covered the stain leaving nothing but the beauty of the winter wonderland.

I thought—that is exactly what God does **when we ask** him to forgive our sin. Not only does he forgive, but he wipes our slate clean. He forgets about it. He doesn't hold it over our heads. Satan loves to bring past sin to mind but God will never bring it up again. Psalm 103:12 says he removes our sin as far as the east is from the west. You see, the east and west will never meet. That's God's way of saying, in essence, out of sight, out of mind.

✧ "Let all that I am praise the LORD; may I never forget the good things he does for me. He forgives all my sins and heals all my diseases. He redeems me from death and crowns me with love and tender mercies. He fills my life with good things." –Psalm 103: 2-5(a)

RSVP TODAY IF POSSIBLE

Jesus Christ requests the honor of your presence in Heaven. You can respond right now.

Simply share the following prayer with God. You may use your own words.

1. **Lord, I admit that I need you.** (I have sinned.)
2. **I want forgiveness for my sins and freedom from eternal death.** (I repent.)
3. **I believe Jesus died and rose from the grave to forgive my sins and to restore my relationship with you.** (I believe in Jesus.)
4. **By faith, I invite Jesus Christ into my life. From now on, I want to live in a loving relationship with Him.** (I receive Jesus Christ as my Savior and Lord.)

✧ "But to all who believed him and accepted him, he gave the right to become children of God." –John 1:12

When you make your decision to accept Jesus Christ, contact a local Bible-believing Christian church for guidance and connection. Ask God to impress upon you which church you should attend.

Read the Bible. A great place to start is the book of John in the New Testament.

Commit to connecting with a church Sunday. You'll find the answers to a lot of your questions as well as a lot of good people with whom you can worship God.

Adapted from the *Louisiana Baptist Message*, February 21, 2008.

Printed in the United States
202625BV00005B/1-144/P